CHILD OF MY CHILD

CHILD OF MY CHILD
Poems and Stories for Grandparents

Edited by Sandi Gelles-Cole and Kenneth Salzmann

Gelles-Cole Literary Enterprises * Woodstock, N.Y. * 2010

Chil of my Child

ISBN 978-0-9786621-2-7

Library of Congress Control Number: 2010932825

Child of My Child: Poems and Stories for Grandparents
Edited by Sandi Gelles-Cole and Kenneth Salzmann

Cover and interior design by Omar Guilarte, Cowdesign.com.

Child of My Child: Poems and Stories for Grandparents is available from
Gelles-Cole Literary Enterprises, P.O. Box 341, Woodstock, NY, 12498
(www.LiteraryEnterprises.com) or online at www.ChildOfMyChild.biz.

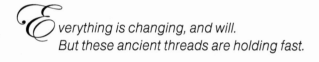*verything is changing, and will.
But these ancient threads are holding fast.*

KAS

ACKNOWLEDGMENTS

The editors are grateful to everyone who assisted in the birth of <u>Child of My Child</u>, including each of the poets and writers who share their voices and wisdom in this book. We also are indebted to designer Ileana Silva-Guasch and her staff, novelist Lucia Nevai for her assistance in preparing the manuscript, Emily Caigan and Khem Caigan for bringing the book to life on the Internet, and all of those who provided, or appear in, the photos for the book cover: Amy Lonas for the photo of Renee Mark and Cory Lonas; Leslee Karol for the photo of herself and her grandchildren; Blake Wilcox for his photo of his father, Dan Wilcox, and his son, Alexander; and Anthony Tassarotti for his photo of Paul Hoagland's grandson, Brayden.

TABLE OF CONTENTS

Publication Credits

Some works in this volume have been published previously in other books and journals:

BABYSKIN: NOTES FOR A GRANDCHILD, appeared in <u>Hapax Legomena</u> by Barbara Adams (Lewiston Poetry Series, The Edwin Mellen Press, 1990).

An earlier version of K. Biadaszewicz's THE SINGER, THE MARTYR, AND ME was included in the anthology, <u>Knit Lit</u>, edited by Linda Roghaar.

CARDINALTHROUGH BIFOCALS by Regina Murray Brault was published in <u>Professional Touch</u> (1999) and <u>Beneath the Skin</u> (2006).

DANCING WITH GRANDPA by Edward M. Cohen appeared in *Child Magazine* (March, 1996).

LEMONS by Barbara Crooker originally appeared in the *Valparaiso Poetry Review*.

RIVER BANK by Darcy Cummings was published in *Natural Bridge* (2005) and in <u>The Artist as Alice: From a Photographer's Life</u>.

GRANDMA ESTHER by Laurie Lee Didesch appeared in *Northeast Corridor*; her poem, GRANDMA SYLVIA, is forthcoming in *Jewish Women's Literary Annual*.

Werner Hengst's essay, LITTLE MISS ENTROPY, appears online at <u>www.WernerHengst.com</u>.

SHE CONVALESCES IN A CHAIR BY THE WINDOW by Pearl Karrer was published in <u>Poets On: Healing</u> and her chapbook, <u>Weathering</u> (Slapering Hol Press).

SHRAPNEL by Janet M. Lewis is included in Getting Kind of Late and Selected Poems by Jan Lewis.

EMANUEL by Naomi Ruth Lowinsky appears in her collection, Adagio and Lamentation (Fisher King Press, 2010).

JACOB, THREE AND A HALF MONTHS OLD, TELLS ME A STORY by Mary Makofske was published in *Calyx: A Journal of Art and Literature by Women* (Summer, 2008).

THE GRANDPARENTS by Larry Rubin was originally published in the *Emory University Quarterly* (Fall, 1966).

Ada Jill Schneider's poem, HEIRLOOM, first appeared in her book, <u>Behind the Pictures I Hang</u> (Spinner Publications, 2007).

TOWERS: CENTURY CITY, LA by Myra Shapiro appeared in River Styx and <u>I'll See You Thursday</u> (Blue Sofa Press, 1996).

Elaine Starkman's APRICOTS FOR ISAAC was included in <u>Dreaming Waking Life: Six Poets, 66 Poems</u> (October, 2000).

BEFORE MY GRANDSON'S SURGERY by Donna Wahlert was published in <u>Mothers & Daughters</u> (June Cotner, ed.).

First
words
By Kenneth Salzmann

*C*HILD OF MY CHILD was born in April, 2009, along with its flesh and blood twin, Josephine, 7 pounds, 6 ounces upon arrival.

In truth, we didn't quite know at the time that a book had been born.

All of our attention was focused instead on one small child who had just reshaped our lives and changed our identities in ways we are still discovering. But it was inevitable that, sooner or later, we would look for a literary response to Josie's life-changing presence, given our own backgrounds and sensibilities.

For me, Josie's birth brought the seemingly straightforward passage into grandparenthood. That joy, however, was necessarily tempered by the awareness that her Grandmother Diana, my wife of nearly thirty years, did not live to see our only child become a father. For Sandi, who is now my wife, Josie brought joy as well, along with a flood of questions about the place she would have in Josie's life as a step-grandmother.

We realized then that being a grandparent in the 21st century brings both timeless joys and sometimes harrowing challenges. Families fracture and recombine, often muddying traditional roles. For some, becoming a grandparent also means becoming a caretaker again.

For some, becoming a grandparent is an insistent call to look themselves or their own children in the face and take account. For others, *not* being a grandparent is a kind of loss. For many, that grandchild arrives bundled in equal parts hope and fear, because the baby's parents may have struggled with substance abuse, financial or legal problems, or other demons. Sometimes, people become grandparents, but only learn that fact years later, as one poem here explores.

And, perhaps for all, the arrival of a new generation brings undeniable evidence of aging and mortality. That may be a particularly tough pill to swallow for the millions of Baby Boomers who have aged into this new role (and sometimes bristle at taking on traditional grandparent names).

When we decided to create this anthology and began soliciting contributions, Sandi and I suspected that some of these issues and concerns would be reflected and examined in the work we would receive. The mountain of submissions we received, however, brought many unexpected stories, too—along with much more excellent material than we possibly could use in a single volume. In assembling the collection, we have been blessed to have the always wise, sometimes surprising, sometimes challenging, prose and poetry of more than five dozen highly accomplished writers as our building material.

We are grateful to each of them and proud to include their work in CHILD OF MY CHILD.

That title, by the way, is borrowed from a wonderfully resonant image offered up, in slightly different forms, by two contributors to this volume: Barbara Evers and Karen Neuberg. It is both a powerful image in its own right and a fitting umbrella for the wide range of experience and emotion contained in this book.

Babyskin:
notes for
A grandchild

By Barbara Adams

At first, you will get all that you want—
   milk, sleep, softness, warmth,
   and love for nothing.
Then, gradually, you will get to know
   pain, fear, disgust, loneliness
through your soft babyskin.

For a long time, if you are a lucky one,
   you will enjoy timeless fun—
   running, throwing, singing, skipping,
and giggling in the dark game of hide and seek.
For a long time, if you are a lucky one,
   the worst you will suffer is broken
   skin or bone, the fever of a cold
   and happy goosebumps.

Then, precious heir, suddenly one day
   Time begins
and you will want what you can't always get—
   lobster, French wine, down bed, cradling arms,
   love for nothing.
You will try to keep what can't be saved—
   joy, peace, content, and soft
   babyskin.
You will come down with the chronic fever,
   incurable, the weariness and chill
   of a broken promise, a frozen dream,
   and the thrill of a breakable heart.

Finally, my innocent descendant, you will learn to sing
   (if you're an heir of mine)
   of pain, disgust, hate, and loneliness.
But you will not be afraid if you know all this
   and love someone—or two—for nothing.
You will live, then, as well as can be expected
   till your babyskin is tough as mine.

Child of my Child

Daughter

By Christine Allen-Yazzie

She loves my daughter
As she wishes she'd loved me

Idle hands
Falling over small brown arms

Lego stables putting up
A dozen pretty pink ponies and a cat

She loves my daughter
And I can't get enough

Hot buttered carrots
Alongside sweet halibut

Can't get enough

Soothing songs of farm animals and stars
I can't recall

She loves my daughter
And when she doesn't

When she doesn't

There go the planets
Swirling by
Shopkeepers and gardeners and dentists and the like

I am the one with the black mouth
The one who can't say her name
Without saying it slowly, in vain

I am her pain
I am the cost
The lost years
An injured neck
A wandering husband

I am blustery winters
Another room

I am the one who looks away
Who doesn't speak kindly to strangers
Who rarely speaks to friends

Who has a daughter!
The one given a ring
Who lost the ring
In the curtains
Who lost a fistful of hair
In the curtains
I am the curtain

There she is!
Pointing at the talking bird— *Dat*
Pointing at the fruity plate— *Dat*
Pointing at a stool— *Dat*

I am my mother's daughter-bearer
I am my mother's—
I am a daughter
I am a bearer or daughter

I am a girl sitting on the couch
Watching my little one pick
A zebra Band-Aid off her leg
My girl, she had shots today
She exhales
An exquisite whimper

Child of my Child

My mother, it is for her I bring my—
It is for her

Try it again

I bring my daughter
To love
I love her

I love her as I wish
I love her as I will

I love my daughter
I love my daughter
As I wish I loved
As I might have loved
As I could very well

Of course I love my mother
I am my mother's daughter

Ode to
grandparenthood
By Diana M. Amadeo

I watch as my grown daughter buries her head in the baby's belly and covers it with kisses. He begins to giggle uncontrollably. While he is in good humor, she slips him into the infant swing and kisses him some more.

The phone rings. My daughter gives me a peck on the cheek, and hands me the phone as she heads out the door to work.

The normally bubbly vibrant voice that I had listened to all of my life now spoke slowly over the telephone. As she talked across the miles, her voice sounded sad, broken and defeated. My eighty-year old mother seemed more than just tired. Her days of literally running circles around me were gone. It wasn't age that was getting my mother down it was my dad.

"Do you know what your father did yesterday?" my weary octogenarian mother asked. "He left to go to the bank at one in the afternoon. By six o'clock he wasn't home so I called your brother. He drove around town for hours trying to trace Dad's path. Your dad couldn't be found so we notified the police. At 2 a.m. I got the call that he had been found. The police asked that we go retrieve him and the car. He had gotten lost and was four hours away. By 6:30 a.m. we were back home and now he is in bed. I've been too upset to sleep. Could this confusion be serious?"

I had noticed that Dad was slowing down. So had my brother. We had talked to Mom about Dad's aging but she refused to see what was apparent to outsiders. Dad's hearing loss to Mom was "proof he doesn't listen to me." His forgetfulness she met with rolled eyes. Dad's aging seemed more frustration to Mom than actual concern. That is, until now.

"Yes, this confusion could be serious, Mom," I replied with a sigh. "Take away his car keys. Explain to Dad he shouldn't drive anymore. We need to get him to the doctor. I'll make a plane reservation to get out there this weekend."

She tries to muffle it, but I can hear the sobs. My heart sinks. My mother never cries. When there is a problem, she grits her teeth, pulls her petite frame tall and carries on. I wish I could wrap my arms around her tiny shoulders and give her a hug.

Child of my Child

Then there was a cry more of a scream from the nearby infant swing. "I gotta go, Mom. My grandbaby is awake and your granddaughter isn't off work for another eight hours." I sigh again, ready to tear-up myself between the crying great grandmother and my own screaming grandbaby.

I call these moments my BLT sandwich. "Blessed Little Trials" describes my position being in the midst of needy generations. I didn't expect life to be like this while still supporting my last child in college. But the older children marry and have children of their own, making their own grandparents great and their parents grand.

And life goes on.

"It is so hard to see Dad this way," my normally stoic mother says. I swallow hard. She was always brave, strong, and mighty. A lady of small stature and build, but nicknamed "firecracker," my mother was the consummate mother and energetic grandmother. Just watching her run up and down stairs, tend to gardening and fixing huge meals, managed to tire people half her age. Dad often was on the sidelines, the quiet observer with a mischievous smile like the all-knowing sage who watches but refuses to interfere with life around him.

I don't want to hang up the phone. But I must with a promise to call tonight. And then I cringe. Tonight I must do my work; two freelance articles are nearing deadline. Sigh.

A grandmother's work is never done.

My husband pops up from his work office downstairs. I relay to him my parents' plight as he tries to pacify the grandbaby. Handing the infant back to me, he heads back to the office, promising to make my plane reservation.

A later phone call that evening found my father oblivious to all the commotion he had caused. Cheerful and talkative, he did acknowledge getting lost (darn all those new roads), but was neither apologetic nor seemingly embarrassed. Nor was he willing to surrender the keys. Was he in denial or stubborn? Previously, I gave him a cell phone that he forgot or refused to carry. I try to be gentle with my father's feelings about squashed independence, but voice my concern for his welfare and anyone else that may be on the road.

As he answered my repeated questions I could envision those beautiful long salt and pepper eyelashes my mother frequently joked are "being wasted on a man" fluttering coyly. I love my Dad. Love him warts and all. Darn it.

Talking to my father confirmed that a visit was necessary. My mother, brother and I would have a family pow-wow about dad after I flew into town. This was not going to be easy. Trips back home were getting harder and harder.

The next day it seemed like my grandson could sense my anxiety. Just nine months old, he laughed and giggled as I smothered him in kisses and then voiced displeasure when I put him on the floor to crawl around. When he watched me retrieve the suitcase from the closet, he broke into sobs.

"Hey honey, Grandma has to fly out to check on your great grandparents," I say as if he understands. He finds some lint on the floor to explore and crying ceases. I commence to pack.

My husband enters the bedroom and gives me a quick peck to the cheek. He encourages his grandson to crawl from the room so packing can continue uninterrupted. I appreciate the helpful gesture.

Then, I suddenly remember a half century before, my mother scooping my crawling brother off the floor and smothering him in kisses as he giggled uncontrollably.

Life seems to repeat itself.

Parenthood/Grandparenthood/Great grandparenthood....the cycle of life.

Eviction

By Lynore Banchoff

The snails appeared at night
along narrow brick lit
by the moon. They, too, trailed

silver paths, but crackled under my feet.
Some survivors found shadows
among the Calla Lilies near

the French doors where an apple
had fallen from the grasp
of two-year-old Natalie. Her teeth

had broken the skin, the flesh lay
ripe. In the morning, she squatted next
to a snail anchored in satisfaction

or self-defense, grabbed the shell,
and left behind the jellied body detached
like the mass of a whale flung

upon a shelf of rock. It was half
gone, its castle between her fingers,
antenna retracted,

its central meeting place of glistening
flesh and home severed
while the apple remained

succulent, available to others sure to inch
along the narrow brick, casting silver
beneath their bodies.

The Newborn
Grandchild

By Helen Bar-Lev

*Y*ou were born one early January noon
That transformed me into grandparenthood
Skinny little bundle of perfection
I was the first one to greet you
Into this imperfect world

We conversed – I with words
You with your senses
A bond formed then,
As tight as the swathing clothes
As beautiful as your eyes
Roaming the room,
Eyebrows puckered
Questioning the sensations
Of a world outside the womb

Conversation ended
Mother recovered,
You reverted back to her care

Tiny enchantress
Who could have imagined
You'd snuggle so securely
Into that unsuspecting compartment
Of my heart, vacant and aching for you
All these years.

Child of my Child

The singer,
the Martyr,
And Me
By K. Biadaszkiewicz

*B*ecause of the double shifts there was no time and no room for a cafeteria, so I walked over to my grandmother's house for lunch, since she lived only a couple of blocks from the school. You could tell which house was hers because even while you were still on the sidewalk, before you turned toward the rambling front porch, most of the time you could hear her practicing her chords.

My father's mother was a teacher of voice and piano, the only girl of thirteen children, raised on a Pennsylvania farm. To feed the family and the hired men, she and her mother baked forty loaves of bread a week and twenty pies. It was my grandmother's special job to clean all the chamber pots and work the garden, and she was glad when it rained so she could sew. Late at night, exhausted, she would retreat to the piano and practice, dreaming of one day becoming an opera star.

She caught something called a social disease from the brute her daddy made her marry, and, when the doctor told her she would die unless he removed all her female organs, she told him she would just as soon die.

She ran away to New York City, stole my grandfather from his common law wife and children, and made the headlines as The Singing Mother, raising four boys while getting rave reviews for her coloratura recitals at Town Hall.

She liked her Campbell's chicken noodle with chopped hard-boiled egg, but I preferred mine plain, and all through those long-ago lunches, she used to tell me about how good she was, how hard she worked, how beautifully she sang, and how men had only one thing on their minds. She refused to be referred to as Grandmother, insisting on "Nanny".

My mother's mamusz ran away, too, from German occupied Poland, to Milwaukee, where she and Djadja struggled to raise their four little girls, never for a moment forgetting the baby who died in Poland or the little boy who was stillborn after two days and nights of hoping, in the upstairs of a duplex on the south side. She was, they say, the best cook in Milwaukee, but when there was no money for groceries and a cupboard empty except for a little flour, she would serve her family a paste of flour and water, and weep.

When I was younger and unbelievably stupid, it used to trouble me that neither of my grandmothers matched the ones in the stories or in the movies. I was embarrassed, like it was somehow my fault that out of all the kids in school I was the only one whose grandmothers didn't bake me cookies and knit me sweaters. One day in second grade I was standing in the lavatory line when the girl behind me tapped me on my shoulder.

"You going to your grandmother's again for lunch?

"I do every day." It felt good to say that there was something that happened every day, something I could count on.

"She nice?"

"Yes," I said. "She and my grandfather have a little house in the woods."

"What woods?"

"Farther than you can see," I said. "My grandfather builds little wooden dolls, and my grandmother knits little clothes for them."

I didn't see it as a lie. I saw it as honoring how it should be.

That's why I ran away, to make things the way they were supposed to be. I learned how to crochet. I learned how to knit. I learned how to make warm, flavorful chipatis from nothing but flour and water. I baked bread, made pies, and discovered the secret of life.

If you make a mistake knitting, you have to start over, but in crocheting you merely rip out your mistake and proceed.

The difference between flour-and-water soup and crisp, fragrant chapatis is the difference between ripping everything up or staying with it, looking at it another way, working at it, looping and pulling, pulling and looping again, trusting that every stitch somehow, someday, might make a difference.

Child of my Child

Cardinal
Through Bifocals

By Regina Murray Brault

From the crust of the
white lie of winter,
what I thought was my
grandson's red mitten
took flight.

The Letter
she finds
After my death

For Jessica
By Clinton B. Campbell

*T*he gods say a single butterfly
fluttering its wings mid-Atlantic
will cause a Pacific monsoon.
Jessica, you are that butterfly,
two days old cocooned in pink,
already the Ariel of our family.

As you leave the hospital
I fumble with the mail,
find my first old age check.
It is a reminder I want
to write this letter and tell you
a little about us your grandparents
in case our time together
may be far too short.

I drink my coffee black,
an old habit from my Army days.
I do the wash, Bubbi irons,
the windows are up for grabs.
We wear the same size pants
and if I find one missing
I know it's in her closet.

We cheat at pinochle.
If I see her touch her ring
she's strong in diamonds
or taps the table, then its clubs.
I probably won't be at your wedding
or meet your first boyfriend.
I know I would like him.
I know your father won't.
Fathers are like that.

Years from now Jessica,
when I'm looking down from heaven
and see a graceful butterfly,
causing chaos in the cosmos,
I will rejoice and proclaim,
"Flutter those wings, Jessica,
flutter those wings."

Child of my Child

While riding
the Gloucester Hammock
I think about mortality

By Sherry Gage Chappelle

Don't picture some ropy, lacy item
slung from two trees and waving
in a Carolina breeze, this is serious
boat bedding styled from New England
fishermen, rigged from our porch rafters
just the way Dad hung it fifty years ago.

On another porch he sat with his mother
swapping tales of family borne on the breeze,
gone like Steven whose face is still sixteen
in my head, who left thirty years of bread ties
in a drawer, who banked his sperm,
grew earthworm farms.

I pump the hammock, push against
the floor, tack from yesterday to today
to tomorrow. One small grandboy sleeps,
head on my breastbone. Outside a fallen bird
flutters to right itself. We want to be
gods, but must settle for keeping our balance
on the uneven boards of general store
lives filled with Band-Aids, quilting thread,
and dried blueberries the color of this craft.

A real
grandmother

By Elayne Clift

"*You're not my real grandma,*" *she told her maternal grandmother when she was four, on an annual visit to a country halfway around the world.* "*Bubbe's my real grandma!*"

I laughed as her mother related the story upon their return, even as I felt a pang of guilt for the pain the comment must have caused.

She has been "my girl" since the day she was born. I taught, counseled, emotionally supported, and then grew to love her mom, first my student and later my unofficially adopted daughter who came from a country I'd known and loved.

Every year for ten years now she has come with her parents to our home for Christmas, where together – Christian, Jew, and Muslim – we celebrate together a time of family and connection, of gratitude for having blessed each other's lives. When my husband and I travel south to the city where they live, we eat ethnic food, play games, tell funny stories, provide advice, and crawl into bed with our girl, who has become the smartest kid I know. Her kindness and generosity make me proud, her jokes make me laugh, her questions challenge me.

I sang to her as a baby, played with her as a toddler, taught her how to bake cookies, teased her, corrected and coddled her. I have shopped for her clothes from newborn to size 12. Now I am watching this lovely child morph into a soon-to-be-young woman – "officially a pre-teen," she tells me. I love being her Bubbe.

Neither of my two biological offspring have children; it seems increasingly unlikely that they will, although I continue to hope. The truth is I long for a grandchild that springs from my own womb, my bloodline. Still, I have "my girl," whom I adore. She has given me true joy and I couldn't feel more proud of this child who grows her hair so that she can donate it, who worries about poor people in her native country, who excels in so many ways compassionately and creatively.

Am I a real grandmother? Some might say no, not really. I say yes. Yes! Because it doesn't get more real than this, not emotionally anyway. She is my girl and I am her Bubbe. (It's amazing the things she "gets from me," from being left-handed to getting easily overheated.) In so many ways, now and forever, we are joined at the hip.

And that's enough for both of us.

Dancing
with grandpa
By Edward M. Cohen

*W*hen I pick up my grandson, Noah, he is sullen and silent. His teacher tells me he awoke during naptime crying, in the midst of a bad dream.

I suggest we go to the park near Ruthie's, his old babysitter's house, where Noah used to play before his parents transferred him to pre-school. He doesn't object, so we head that way, and I'm hoping he'll fall back asleep in his stroller.

It's been a difficult year for both of us. My wife died last spring and, since I didn't recover quickly enough, I was dumped from my job. "Early Retirement" it's called.

Over the summer, my son and daughter-in-law, Eric and Liz, spent long weekends with me at the beach house. In return, I did a lot of babysitting. Every afternoon, Noah and I played with Mr. Potato Head, ate cucumber and bologna, emptied my desk drawer and, best of all, danced together on the porch.

We got along so well that his parents and I agreed that Liz could go back to work fulltime since I was free to pick up Noah from pre- school. So they switched him from Ruthie's, which was only a half-day affair, to a structured school that lasts from 9:00 to 4:00. I think they were worried about overburdening me, but a seven hour day is awfully long for a 2 1/2 year old.

And now, Noah has bad dreams in the midst of this group experience where things are run on a strict schedule. He's being rushed into learning about dealing with authority figures and getting along with a roomful of kids. I'm not saying it's bad to learn these lessons, but it's not as good as dancing with your grandpa on the porch.

I offered to pick up Noah earlier than 4:00 because, despite my plans to look for a job or go back to school, I find myself spending most days looking through photos of my wife. But his teachers said my snatching him early would be disruptive to his routine.

How ironic that Noah has too much scheduling in his life and I have too little.

Naptime. Snacktime. Circle Time. We put things away when we're finished. Time to arrive, time to leave, and, oh no, your grandpa arrives early because he has nothing else to do. What kind of a world pushes a child into super-scheduling, only for him to find, when he's 58, that he can't fill the days by himself?

Noah doesn't fall asleep on the way to the park. He wants to go on the tire swing and I push him for an eternity. At last, he starts to talk about how he was scared at school, how he can't wait until his birthday, and how he hopes to get a monkey.

On the swing, he figures out that, school or no school, he'll still have times with Grandpa – when he's allowed to swing for hours until his fears and worries can come tumbling out.

Eventually, he agrees that it is time to go. I lift him from the swing and can feel that he wants to stay in my arms. So I pat his back, he lays his head on my shoulder, and I walk him back and forth, singing in his ear – just like my wife did to his father decades ago.

And when he has had enough, he pops his head up, looks at my face, and we smile.

Lemons

By Barbara Crooker

A yellow sun splashed lavish light
on the garden, a bright bloom
of a morning, full of possibility.
I was away from home, teaching,
when one of the poems peeled
away the thin rind of memory,
and there I was, back
in the maternity ward
when my firstborn died.

I remember how white and cold
the room was, even though
my friends brought flowers:
irises, roses. I was hollow,
a fruit that had been pulped
for juice, leaving nothing
but a shell, no flesh, no seeds.

Thirty years later, my daughter's
globed stomach, and then, there
was Daniel, shining and puckered
in the moony glow of the delivery
room, rinsed with light from another
world, and a new day dawning.

River Bank

By Darcy Cummings

My daughter casts off in a raft
woven from my ribs, her swollen belly
pulling her to the current. I said
I'd always care for her, but the cradle
of my fingers is reft. She remembers
the women and babies who drowned on this river;
I told her their names the first time
we came here. Then I delivered her
so easily—nimble amphibian, she slid
from my body like water. But this labor,
this letting go and bringing back,
like a crude gutting, leaves me gasping, banked.

Child of my Child

Grandma
Esther
By Laurie Lee Didesch

You lived red, the color of flushed cheeks after chasing up a hill,
at the top, panting and smiling, heady at the accomplishment,
as I imagine you might have done during your childhood.
In my youth, you brought me a Mandarin doll from Chinatown
in silk and carrying a lantern like the sultry sun rising above
the Bay and a straw purse from Nassau Island stitched
with fingers of yarn, rays of the same brilliant star.

You traveled beyond widowhood and met a former navy
diver. He made you his poster girl, and we called him Bernie.
A favorite photo rings with laughter: the one where
the grandkids piled on his lap, almost tipping an easy chair.
And when bells rang in the New Year, you and Bernie
chased us out of bed with hats and horns and noisemakers
we screeched along with as we twirled their handles.

All this, you must be telling Grandpa Lou, after so many years
apart. I know his soft chocolate eyes from your dresser top,
and how as newlyweds, he held you on the beach through
the hottest summer nights with a breeze off the lake
and sand skimming your legs. We buried those legs in red
slacks. Now, I keep a pair of your well-worn sandals, and they
remind me to keep after my own soles.

Grandma
Sylvia
By Laurie Lee Didesch

*P*reparing your eulogy, the Rabbi consoled
daughter and son, stepchildren, grandchildren,
and each and every one told him with a wink
that they highly suspected being your favorite
by the way you grabbed them round and pressed
them close, while smelling of chicken schmaltz;
treated them to a delectable chocolate rum ball
from Gitel's Bakery around the corner, beamed
at their mere presence and then shook your head
in admiration; you squeezed their sleeping bags
into your cramped apartment for slumber parties
with conversations lasting late into the evening,
and you threw up your arms in solidarity when
they shared their heart-felt secrets; knit for them
in between visitors, an afghan or sweater in pink
and purple or green and orange; adored them all.

Child of my Child

Grandson

By Meredith Escudier

*I*n my dream
I held my grandson tight.
I put my hand on his little naked shoulder
and wrapped my arm around his waist.

In my dream,
we found a magic swimming pool,
turquoise, warm, rectangular, large
and we slipped in together...
sputtering, bouncing, bobbing, gliding.

In my dream,
I made him breakfast
and sat next to him and watched him swallow.
I set him up on the rug to play
and while I did the dishes, I felt
connected to him across the room.

This was my dream and although
in real life, he was faraway,
beyond my touch, living at bay,
I visited him through longing,
a vivid voyage, a chosen foray.

In real life, I carry around a weight
of unused grandmotherly acts,
a whole shopping bag of smiles and
ready vigilance and pie crust know-how,
of art projects and songs to sing
and the desire to cup his head in my hand.
Still, this was my dream and
when I woke up, I felt happy.

Baby
picture
By Meredith Escudier

I put your photograph in
a picture frame but
how strange
your little soft parts are enclosed
in hand-painted Venetian glass
right angles surround your face
squaring off your features
closely capping your pulsing fontanelle
posing supposing limits when
you are not limited not to this moment
and not to this space your
life is commencing your inner life
dancing unbridled prancing you
are a free-flow a torrent a rush
transforming freeforming roaring
a mountain river.

Child of my Child

While
our grandson
Connor
was being born

By Michael Estabrook

uring the 12 long hours that poor Laura struggled
through her labor with Connor, her second child,
her dutiful husband at her side, my wife and I, as dutiful
grandparents, looked after Brooke, their first child.
We watched The Wiggles and Sesame Street on TV, went
shopping at The Rugged Bear for new mittens and boots,
played the tickle game and rolled around on the sofa,
marched from room to room blowing a lovely tune on our
recorders, took naps (Brooke and Bapa), explored every
room in the Children's Discovery Museum (Brooke and
Nana), called Mommy at the hospital 5 times, raked the
leaves beneath the old apple tree, ate noodles, Santa
cookies, strawberries, Cheerios, pineapple, mashed
potatoes, and donuts, played monkey-in-the-middle,
made copies of our hands out of Play Dough, read Elmo
& Friends, The Very Hungry Caterpillar, and the Further
Adventures of Peter Rabbit, took apart and put back
together again the two Russian dolls, thought about putting
the trains back up around the Christmas tree but ran out
of energy, danced to Christmas with the Chipmunks and
Beethoven's Third Symphony, drew some colorful abstract
art with magic markers, took a bunch of ornaments off the
tree and put most of them back on again, and laughed and
laughed and laughed.

Heck of a productive day all in all, wouldn't you say?

Child at my Child

Unexpected

By Barbara Evers

I hoped that my daughter misread the symptoms, that she wasn't pregnant. Not because I didn't want grandchildren, but because of her circumstances. This cherished daughter of mine stumbled onto the wrong path in life in her early twenties and had wandered down a rugged, pot-holed overgrown trail from her misguided choices. She was not ready to be a mother, and I was not ready to handle the responsibility if and when she fell apart.

Her pregnancy forced me to wave good-bye to the freedom my husband and I had come to love and enjoy. Our marriage started with five children, so we greeted our empty nest years with great anticipation.

What I forgot is the power that a baby carries with it. The overpowering, inexplicable surge of unconditional love that I felt with my children was now my daughter's due. I saw it form in her as her due date drew near. Not to say that she did an about-face in her behavior, but her life picked its way back towards a better, more traversable path.

Still I feared her ability to make the right decisions. I grieved over the few medical options available to an unemployed mother-to-be. I cringed when I took her to appointments, afraid to touch anything that came in contact with these people who obviously did not understand the responsibility that their actions required of them.

Then, my granddaughter entered the world.

I could not believe it. I stood by my daughter's bedside while she labored and watched this tiny little girl emerge into the uncertain world of a single parent home.

All parents know that the love we experience prior to parenthood holds a small flame to the force and the power of the love that sweeps into your soul at the birth of your own child. Believe it or not, the birth of your grandchild carries a stronger, more potent love.

This is the child of my child.

You know more of what the world can do to harm her, and you want to protect her from all of it. The knowledge that you can't frustrates you even more, building a stronger will to protect and love.

Because of her mother's circumstances, they lived with us for the first 16 months of my granddaughter's life. This prevented me from spoiling her like most grandparents do with their grandchildren, but I gained something greater. In her world, I became part of the foundation of her life. Her home held Mommy, Babbie (her name for me), and Granddad. Besides her Mommy, we became her favorite people in the world.

Child of my Child

She is now three years old. When I greet her, her grin stretches from ear to ear and she breathes out my name with joy, "Babbie."

When my children were little, I couldn't wait for them to grow up and walk and talk and meet the milestones of childhood. The time flies by even faster now, but this time I beg it to slow down. I want to hang on to those days where she seeks out joy and comfort in us. I hope to be that grandmother who will always be cool and worthwhile to the growing teenager that she will quickly become. I want to be the shoulder she cries on when love lets her down.

But most of all, I want her life to take its time getting us there. I want my sweet, precocious grandchild to have a lifetime of childhood first.

Introduction

By Anne C. Fowler

*A*melia's a hit with all Mother's nurses.
First great-grandchild? She's adorable!
But Mother's skeptical. She clings tight
to her stuffed owl. A comfort in this
strange company.—*Too bad about
the deformity*, she announces. What
is she thinking? What baby, in what decade?
—*Grandma, her name's Amelia*, Liz says
firmly, *want to hold her?* No, she does not,
she has her hands full with this bird.—*Look*,
I tell her, *four generations of family
women all together!* Mother sits up
straighter in her hospital bed.—*That baby's
head is very round*, she says. *I think she'll
be a bowler, a very good one.*

Spirit-Plasma

By Hugh Fox

A New Year's Eve call from
Cambridge, Massachusetts,
"Grandpa, this is Rivka, I'm
Putting together an album of
all the pictures we had taken
together since I was born, and
I want the name of that park
with all the swings next to
a lake…I forget…, "You
sound great…," "Well, I'll
Be fourteen in two weeks, doing
OK, and we'll be with you for
three months beginning in June,"
"Great…the name of the park is
Nirgendwo Park…," she begins
to laugh, her father from Stuttgart,
always pushing her into German
("Just a little cultural frosting,
Nothing political."), "Nirgendwo
Means NOTHING, NOTHING
PARK…"Well, OK, Irgendo
Park
she moves close to
hysterical laughter, "That means
EVERYWHERE…," "OK,
when you're around I'm everywhere,
when you're gone, I'm nowhere…,"
"Like your Czech grandmother in
Cicero, you're like that to me, the
one door I can open without second
thoughts…I even look like you…,"
"And I look like her. Yaksamash?"
"I'm fine, and you…?" "How do
you know any Czech?," "Three
months a year with you for the
last fourteen years…that's a lot
isn't it?" "Not enough."

Buking it

By Hugh Fox

*N*ot exactly feeling suicidal, but with
All the leaves down, clouds as thick as
refrigerator doors, mostly birdless,
retired, just me and my M.D. wife
who spends her days looking at
maybe-cancer-cells, my e-mails
and submissions to mags that
get 500 submissions for every
acceptance and they're looking
for new talent, not voices in the
museum archives, and then daughter
Alexandra (41) comes to visit with
little blonde, blue-eyed Beatrice
(2), not that it wouldn't be the same
if she were black and black-eyed, but
there's a certain traditional angelicness
about her, and she starts hitting me
and laughing, I put on Ibert's Escales
and she starts dancing, I start dancing,
she follows me, in my mind thousands
of hours of balleting, let's try the hands
out and around, a step forward, a step
back, circling, twisting, her following
every movement, then lunch and she
gobbles down my maple-crunch cookies
and then "Sun…park…," out to Harris
Nature Center two miles down the road,
rivers and deer and some trees still
flaming red, "Grandpa…" holding my
hand, "More…more…," wondering,
after I'm dead, will she remember
this/me when she grows up….

Hank Smith:
Walking With Marcy
By Lewis Gardner

*W*hen they moved in with Betty and me
after the divorce, my daughter and *her* daughter,
it annoyed me at first, spoiling our quiet routine,
but soon I enjoyed having everyone together,
especially Marcy running around the place,
asking questions, sidekick on my afternoon walk.

Getting Marcy ready for school became my job.
I'd fix her breakfast and walk her to the school bus.
In winter, wake-up time was dark as midnight.
Why was the morning star so bright, she asked.
In spring the sky could be pink and orange
as she took my hand walking to the road.

Years passed and I saw she was letting go my hand
when the bus came near, averting her eyes
when kids yelled: "Hiya Gramps!"
As we walked to the road one morning, she said,
You know, "Grandpa, it's okay if you want
to sleep late. I can get myself ready."

I looked at her, pretty and grown so much
since first she joined us, and I said not a word,
just nodded and smiled back. I heard the bus
brake to a stop, heard the kids shouting: "Hey Marcy!"
as I started back to the house. I could stay
in bed, sleep as late as I want.

Steps

By Sandi Gelles-Cole

*J*osephine was born 16 months ago, granting a wish I had for my husband to become a grandfather. I confess to the self-serving piece of that desire. I yearned to be a grandmother but I have no children of my own.

For a while I wrestled with the branding of our connection. I had never heard anyone referred to as a step-grandmother. My idea was she would call me whatever she wanted when the time came. Then it became clear that my label would be decided by her parents so it didn't really matter what I was thinking.

What is strictly between me and Josie is our relationship. The poems and stories throughout this book reference the immediate awakening of a force the third generation feels upon the entry of the child onto the planet. It seems the immediate passionate attachment might go even beyond what grandparents felt for their own children. Perhaps it is the mathematics involved, love for child times love for child's child. Through choices made long ago, I will never feel it, but I now have the opportunity to stir up a separate form of feeling.

My husband was the initial conduit. As he held Josie for the first time something passed over him, a falling away. The troubles marking his face, even those that had made me fall in love with him, were erased for the days of Josie's first visit. He was in a different kind of love. There was no ownership. This love was devoid of the struggles that come from caring for another person. For that reason I wanted Josie close to us. She was a healer.

My gratitude for this diapered mush grew warmer as Ken observed his own child in the role of parent. The nurturing his son learned from his parents was in action. The father saw the good job he and the young man's mother had done. So there was this new facet of father/son affection that multiplies (there's the math again) as Joshua grows into fatherhood. My husband sees that he has passed along the lessons learned from his own father, deceased for many years. This assures him that a piece of his father is still here. There is a spiritual rejuvenation going on. There is joy. And my bonding to my step-granddaughter pulls tighter.

The next time we saw Josie she was crawling, out and about, no longer a mush, but now an infant and an explorer. I could crawl with her. She could focus her eyes and smile. I hoped that I was an 'other' to her. When we went back home we sent her a rocking horse and when a video came back of her falling off it wasn't just another YouTube baby clip. She was adorable and part of us.

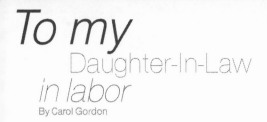

To my
Daughter-In-Law
in labor
By Carol Gordon

*T*hey keep me sitting in the hall
outside your room, outside
the windows glazed
with wire-sandwiched glass,
like a gymnasium.
A second team.

Beige curtains pulled between
the navel of a lamp and me
trying not to hear
efficient shoes of nurses.
Someone sneezes.

Signs say
FIRE   ESCAPE
say   SILENCE

On this bench, alone.
Nothing legitimate to do.
5:32.

Crying begins.

Child of my Child

Grandmother
to the brood
By John Grey

*Y*es, my thoughts don't get around
much anymore,
like my dancing shoes,
my legs, once thought so handsome.
But my blood flows,
not snow-melt quick,
more summer crawl through
drying creek bed.

And there's stuff I still know
and more that I remember,
and it's available to all who
have the patience,
who lean into my meager hearing,
ask the question,
then listen to my wrinkled mouth
for that so hesitant but true response.

For I'm a part of you
for all your lithe and busy bodies.
I drift back from your moment now
into the places you can't see,
report from the past that made you,
that comforts, that provides,
that sustains you going forward.

I grow older,
old as the trees, the mountains,
so you love to whisper.
They don't get around much anymore, either.
But how majestically they stay in place.

Child of my Child

Sunset

By Nancy Gustafson

Tethered to an oxygen tank
Grandpa shuffles across the room,
winds the hollow plastic tube
over his hand in measured loops
precisely as he wound his lariat
when he was a boy of seventeen
and worked as a cowboy for the Ranch.
Grandpa chuckles — *He remembers*

back in nineteen twenty-four
he rode a chestnut Quarter horse,
the envy of all the young ranch hands.
With a piggin' string in his clenched teeth,
he spurred Old Joe to cut out a heifer,
lassoed the bawling maverick,
leaped off Joe in a cloud of dust,
wrestled down and hog-tied the critter.

Plastic lariat under control — *He sighs*
Grandpa circles in baby steps
to position his backside perfectly,
then plops into his worn recliner,
inhales the comforting smell of leather—
a familiar saddle where he snoozes.

Grandpa snores — *He dreams*
of an orange sun in a turquoise sky,
the heady musk of tack and horses,
wiry bodies of sweaty cowboys
molded into rocking chairs
lined up on a bunkhouse porch,
clackety-rock of warped boards,
the light-hearted laughter of callow boys
unmindful of the precious day
vanishing behind magenta mountains.

Life packed with years of cool mornings
burning afternoons, twilight shadows
midnight mysteries, nothing left undone.
Grandpa discerns the circle clearly,
sees the mountain loom before him,
eager to explore the valley on the other side,
where the silver cord unsnapped,
windows are not dimmed, the lantern
of his memory remains aglow. There,
water from the fountain fills the golden bowl.
Grandpa is not afraid — *He knows*

Child of my Child

Little
miss entropy
By Werner Hengst

*S*omewhere between their second and third birthdays, toddlers are said to go through an "orderly" stage. Everything has to be precisely in its place and they get very upset at any disorder. My granddaughter, Eliza, who will be three next month, may have gone through such a stage but, if she did, it was so short that nobody noticed.

Right now, she is in a prolonged phase of disorder. I call her Little Miss Entropy. Entropy is a concept used by cosmologists to describe the gradual running down of the universe. Every time a candle burns, a stream rushes down a mountainside, a meteor streaks across the sky, entropy increases. Things that were bound up in a relatively orderly structure become scattered and randomly distributed. Maximum entropy is reached when all the matter and energy has been degraded into a state of inert uniformity.

Whenever little Eliza passes by, entropy takes a giant step forward. A box of crayons quickly becomes scattered not only over the whole table-top, but on the floor surrounding the table and soon in every room of the house. The cushions of an easy-chair disappear from their supporting structure and magically re-materialize in an upstairs bedroom. The ingredients of a dried-fruit platter disperse all over the house: an apricot here, a shriveled pear there, a white piece of dried pineapple on the armrest of the family room sofa. In seconds, a neat spool of red ribbon becomes a meandering helix that snakes all the way through the kitchen, dining room and living room.

Eliza is a dedicated entropist. Smiling cherubically and softly cooing to herself, she attacks her work with the energy of a piece-worker who has a quota to meet. She is darn good at it, too. It takes her no more than five seconds to dismember a spring-loaded clothes-pin and to scatter its parts so they would never again meet up with each other. With infinite patience, she scissors a piece of Christmas wrapping paper into confetti no bigger than a finger nail and sprinkles it all around the room. And then there are the infamous red rubber bands. They belong to an educational toy consisting of a peg-frame across which the bands are to be stretched to make various designs. Within days, we find red rubber bands everywhere: on the stairs, in our bed, on the bathroom counter, even in the refrigerator. The peg-frame is still awaiting its first design.

Like all hard-working professionals, Little Miss Entropy sometimes takes a break from her labors. For a solid half hour I watch her as she constructs daring towers and bridges from a Lego-like set of plastic components. Her tousled blonde head bent forward, she sits with intense concentration, trying out new ideas. "And this purple tower goes on top of this car…uh, oh, it broke…it's got to go over here…now it fits…and here is a man in a boat under this bridge…and this yellow train is pushing the other train…" all in the same soft baby voice she uses to talk to her favorite toy piggie. At the end of the session, of course, she remembers what her real job is and dashes everything apart.

After visiting for three weeks, Eliza and her family left this morning. Already, the house is beginning to return to its normal old fogy orderliness. Already, I miss her. I miss the level gaze of her gray eyes. I miss her stubby nose and her round pouting lips. I miss her sweet little voice when she says "Granddaddy, read me a story." I miss the way she puts her soft arms around my neck and snuggles her head into the hollow between my shoulder and my ear as we read another book about Curious George. And I miss her little hands, pink and cold from snowball-making, as they creep into my gloves next to mine.

I go upstairs to my office to catch up on a few things I've let slide, and there, on my computer keyboard, sits one of Little Miss Entropy's red rubber bands. I guess she is still on the job.

Riffs
on Samantha
By Barbara Hoffman

for my granddaughter
three-years-old

At Sipp'n'Soda
she stands in the booth
leans against the mirrored wall
I feed her small bites
of chicken tenders
she leans against me
looks over into the next booth
smiles at the people eating
turns to look at the flies
at the top of the mirror

all this while
she's been singing
very softly
I concentrate on listening
"shoo fly, don't bodder me"
"shoo fly, don't bodder me"

Years
from now
By Louise Jaffe

Years from now
when your brain and ears have bloomed
        enough
to weave noises
into tapestries of sense
they will tell you
(as most parents do)
how your twin
was a New York City transit strike
when they'd been expecting
only you.

Years from now
when you're too busy
even to feign listening
(as most children are)
they will tell you
(as most parents do)
how your mommy and daddy
and recently widowed grandma from
    New Jersey
and birthing coach
trekked as if on eggs
through ten blocks of December
to the hospital where you arrived
sans pain killers
three hours later.

Years from now
when you're too fairy-taled
to understand such ugliness
they will tell you how
two sets of divorced, then remarried
    grandparents

Child at my Child

first met you on separate dates
to avoid the strain
of play-acting pleasantries.

Years from now
when years have past-tensed all of
      them
you will be spilling every drop of
      this
for someone none of us
will ever do more
than imagine.

Borrowed
shoes

By David James

"*I*t's also necessary
to be dying"
  Tadeusz Rozewicz

i forget this, among all the rushing and working, chores
and eating, the dressing, the appointments, the laundry.
i'm at that age when i need to start dying
in earnest. with exercise and meds, i might have thirty more
years to make my presence known—write that epic poem,
travel through ireland, mold myself into a memory
my grandchild will recall with kindness.
it's not fair: after a half-century on solid dirt,
i now have my bearings, i know the territory.
the morning frost calls my name; the sunset feels like home.
just when i get comfortable in my skin, no longer a guest
in borrowed shoes, the end rises in the night sky
like a second moon, a dim spotlight i can't escape.
so i start dancing for no particular reason, slow and grotesque,
auditioning for a part in the unknown.

Child of my Child

Choices

By Sheila Golburgh Johnson

I know you're a modern woman,
yet you don't know what you destroy
if you destroy the ball of cells
in your womb.

You destroy the blessing of love
from my son whom you think
you love –

my son who wants to marry you
and bring up the child
with devotion.

What changed your mind, sweet girl
who was so sure of her mind?

You are a glowing planet
tangled in his branches.

I open my arms to enfold you.

We do not take death lightly.

Our Talmud says
One who saves a child
saves the world.

Child of my Child

She convalesces
in a chair
by the window

By Pearl Karrer

*M*y grandmother's arms,

more and more transparent
like the petals on her white
moth orchid wasting
to sheer tissue
held together by capillaries,

cross on her lap,

summer Mondays I wake
to yeast and cinnamon
wafting up the stairwell,
feel my saliva
rush as I enter
her kitchen, accept
my snippet of dough.

We knead to the slap,
sigh of the loaf, my child
wrists and hands fighting
for rhythm beside her smooth
tempo—knuckle roll, wrist
drop, quarter turn. Flour
creeps up our arms,

hands, palms down,

pummel my back, panic
rising past my thin
shoulder blades. Without
air, I rasp and gurgle.
She flips me
upside-down and a lemon drop
dislodges, skittering
across the linoleum,

Child of my Child

only her fingers flutter recognition;

    drawn like a moth
    to her Mason and Hamlin, light
    spilling onto the bench;
    my feet, at first, not
    touching the floor, she stacks
    phone books beneath them,
    settles beside me to underpin
    rhythm and harmony while I press
    treble keys, their ivory yellowed
    by age and the oil
    from her students' hands;

reaching out, my hands—the same

    long fingers, short nails,
    knuckles thickened by études
    and kneading, the gold band
    too new to feel natural,

cup over hers

    as if to return
    all she has given me.

Mary
Nedvedova Havel
By Charlene Langfur

My grandmother Mary moved to New Jersey from Prague in 1897.
She started her small farm there in a town called Little Ferry.

What is now the Meadowlands, across from Manhattan, Little Ferry
was backwater country then, home to the best farmland in America,
a garden state, a place of deep loose dark soil where any seed grew.

For years I've tried to find out more about her. I've looked for bits
pieces, scraps of information that showed what she thought of life.

Often I mistake her for someone else, a photo in a magazine.
Always I want her missing words, the ones she didn't leave behind
to mean more than they do, more than they actually can.

People who read Slavic are confused by the Bohemian dialect.
So, I can understand why more of her words weren't saved.
She was, I am told, a simple farmer who chose to express little in words.

But she is clear in the photographs. In them she's small.
Her faced weathered, the babushka drawn tight against her cheeks.

Her eyes seem closed. She is squinting. She is tired. She is shy.
In the pictures she is infinitely tired, bending low.

In the photos I can see that even if her letters were readable,
I might not know what she thought was beautiful or dire or infinite.

Some of her words come to me by word of mouth. Her favorite
phrase was, "Even a blind pig finds an acorn once in a while."

She taught her children this phrase. They learned it in Bohemian.
Her son, my father, taught it to me in English, "Remember the acorns," he said.

He watched the pigs eat them. That's why he held them in his hand like treasures.
For years I collected acorns like pennies for luck. The acorn was a sign.

Child of my Child

I do not know how she learned the phrase. I think about her as a young woman
on the farm outside of Prague where each day she swept the dirt floor with a broom.
She swept the pebbles and the dirt out the front door, sprinkling the rest with water.

Always she lived around pigs and chickens. She saw some acorns now and then
and she smiled. This is what I think happened. She saw them and she smiled
Maybe the phrase about the pig was handed back to her. She also
collected last lines.

Maybe she collected acorns for luck because of the person who came before her.

I know she had different reasons for saving or not saving what she wrote.
Writing in Slavic Bohemian was forbidden for many years. Her dialect was unacceptable.

Czechoslovakia, as she called it, was occupied for 1,500 years on and off.
The Mongolians were there first, the Hungarians, eventually the Germans again and again.

In her lifetime, birth, marriage, death certificates, diplomas were written in German,
a language she never understood well. She was a farmer and she never went to school.

Yes, so she, my grandmother, was a farmer. She raised chickens and pigs
and she grew vegetables. She gave birth to thirteen children. She survived.

She plucked chicken feathers endlessly. In winter she wrapped her children in the feather
comforters and placed hot fired bricks in them to keep them warm.

In the cold of so many winters she looked out on the Hackensack River where she drew
her water and she thought it was beautiful and light and blue.

Today the river is black, dangerous, full of sludge, chemicals from Clifton, oil, garbage.
I know she loved the river where her children, those who survived birth, swam and played.
I don't think she thought about Prague then or any of the troubles—when she was at the river.

So, she lived by the blue river and she was taciturn, strong, always diligent and hard working.
It was her style. She was practical. She was, above all, a survivor.

The seven Czech farms that made up little Ferry then are mostly land fill now.
The Meadowlands, once a wetland, gradually became a vast dump, where
for most of my life time garbage was trucked in hour after hour, night and day.

From Newark in the south to Hackensack in the north, a line of endless dumps,
came to mark the fertile farmland that once enriched this whole area of Jersey.

I watched both the filling of the wetlands and the sinking of it also.
A stadium, a race track, condominiums, an arena, now sit atop it all.

These days the immense wetland shoreline of garbage landfill with development atop
slowly sinks as all things built on
unsolid ground eventually do.

Some folks in Manhattan still buy and sell letters written by farmers like Mary Havel,
my grandmother. The letters are used to construct histories, data about the old farms,

the truth about the culture and the wisdom and the business of the area more than a
century ago. For them garbage is a separate issue as developers build stuff on top of it all.
I don't think my grandmother would have understood this.

I see our family name in the newspaper now. Vaclav Havel became the president
of a free Czechoslovakia and he led the way to a free eastern Europe.

For me, Havel stands for my grandmother, farmer, lover of land, mother of 13 children.
If you stand at the edge of the Meadowlands you can see what has come to pass.
No matter how hard or how long you look, you can't see the end of it.

You can't see how far, how endless the dump actually is—of wrecks, cars, refuse, rust,
cadmium, arsenic, parts of trucks, girders, building parts covered up. I have no words to
explain this.

Nearby the path where she dragged her vegetable wagon
by hand from Little Ferry up toward the Hudson is now the Jersey Turnpike.

When I was a child, people from Ridgefield and smaller river towns remember the wagon
and the small stooped woman who rang her bell by hand as she walked.

The meadowlands where her children picked strawberries for 5 cents an hour during the
big war are filled with mercury, old tires, wood beams, paper, paint, junk, more junk.

Always I've tried to find the words to explain this. I've none.
So I stick with her words, words we write together somehow, "acorns, quietly I collected
acorns."

Shrapnel

By Janet M. Lewis

Shrapnel, a grenade exploding,
my family has blown itself apart,
to Texas, Jersey, Ohio, Penn's Woods.
Explosions hurt.

Now in searing, secondary explosions,
their families are flying apart to colleges
and jobs across our huge country.
Explosions hurt.

You can't complain. You exploded
from your parents' nest, and they from theirs,
they from theirs, and they from theirs,
back to explosions that crossed oceans.

Explosions hurt.

In the Garden

By Naomi Ruth Lowinsky

or Obie

In your new house—painted shades
of sunlight and sky—there are many rooms
and windows that contemplate

summer hills, the bay.
Your little brother clatters from playroom
to living room to kitchen over shining floors.

You show me your garden, its secret
hiding places, the apricot
brimming with fruit and your own

personal apple tree. You give me a taste
of the tart green fruit; we talk of death—
my father's, and that of Florence

the Great Dane. "She stopped breathing"
you tell me. "Did your father
stop breathing too? Why?"

You are not yet four.
I pray that this house
with its filtered light,

its many rooms that remember
other lives, will protect you. Long
may your parents and your brother

breathe, long may you taste
the fruit of both trees
in the garden.

Child of my Child

Emanuel

By Naomi Ruth Lowinsky

On the day you descended into our world   circles within
circles opened   one hundred and fifty thousand
people marched up Market street   to protest a wrong war
not in our name   not in your name Emanuel   they chanted
and the drag queens of the city came out beautiful in their highest
heels their sleekest black velvet   and they thanked us so much
for coming out to say   "no blood for oil"   "war is not healthy
for children and other living beings"   and an old man on rollerblades
gave yellow roses to the little girls   and a woman bared her very pregnant
belly with a peace sign painted upon it   and i spoke every hour
on my cell phone to your mother to find out how close
were her pains   it was a few hours before your dark head
would crown   your broad shoulders twist out and that glistening coil
of your cord from the other world which your father cut
while your mother cried out to behold you   old wisdom
still clinging about you   Emanuel   it was the day after the full moon
in Capricorn   and the people had awakened to the gathering armies   the gulf
upon which we all teetered   and returned to the streets as we had
when your mother was my baby girl   and we walked up Market street

                                                to protest a wrong war

Emanuel   you have descended   and the world is so new   your first poop
is big news and your good latch   upon your mother's breast   you are
so sweet so calm a being   released from forever to sing among us

                                        little house of God
                                        may we deserve you

Jacob,
three and a half months old,
tells me a story

By Mary Makofske

*Y*ou have been sleeping all afternoon
thinking up this story, which begins
with a trill in the throat, breaks into
gutturals rocking through a grin.

Then your lips purse to a beak, cooing,
each vowel a word, the words strung
into sentences you know to punctuate
with a shift in pitch and a pause.

I know this is a narrative,
the pace breaking from calm
afternoon to rambling dialogue
to danger and a narrow escape.

I begin to recognize vocabulary,
syntax, know when you repeat
for emphasis, or use parallel
structure with synonymous words.

The sound of sense, I think, Frost's
theory about the music of a poem,
the rise and fall, whisper and thrust
of conversation muffled by a wall.

My task is to be the good listener,
slipping *Um hmmm* or *Really*? or *Oh*!
into a gap, or keeping the silence
you insert to build the suspense.

When your brow furrows and the story
stalls, I know to repeat what you've said
so you know I've heard. And you're
watching to see that I follow, want to learn

what sounds make my eyes wide.
Neither you nor I will remember
this story. Only that you told it.
Only that I listened.

Child of my Child

Zachary
discovers stones

By Mary Makofske

What are they, scattered
everywhere, such wealth.
He captures
between thumb and finger
one tawny pebble,
carries it to the curb
and sets it down.
Above, gray clouds
race across blue sky—
but here's another
brown and sharp-edged—
a gift for me, and now
another, set on the curb,
beginning a collection
that even broken macadam
can join, a category
separate from leaves and sticks.
So this is what walking
leads to, bending down
to find what's small, of no
value unless noticed,
his attention polished
like some rare gem.

Child at my Child

Breaking
the code

By Arlene Mandell

I want him to speak our language, but for now he delights in the rhythms of his own, needing no words when he reaches for the fire engine on the shelf above his head or for a bite of the fudge cookie in my hand.

At my laptop, he wiggles his toes, then presses keys. "A," he says. "F" and his silky hair flutters as he blows a line of Fs across the screen. "Zzzzzzzzz," he says, drawing out the sound, pleased with the effect.

Suddenly bored, he wanders off to find the cat.

"Do you want a piece of apple?" I offer. He swivels his head in three quick turns, then pushes the slice toward my mouth.

"It's delicious," I say, taking a bite.

"Apple," he says and grins.

My daughter
has brought me
her baby to love

By Rochelle Mass

I gather things to give them, foggy December mornings
with sour plum jam. By noon I give them hills
with bellies free of clouds and greens polished
by a winter sky.   Pines comb their needles for this
child but her mother wants no more than to drink
coffee in my kitchen, watch me smooth the skin
of her small girl and fold her clothes.

I tell her child what she'll find in the next rainbow
and how we'll splash color on rabbits and a duck
and I hear my daughter listening. I tell the child
about dark birds just over the top of the mountain
and white ones that fly our way on fine days
that glow with clarity
her mother only now has found.

Wild lilies, I tell the little child are like you now,
look over there beside the big rock, I tell her
because she listens as her mother never did.
Listen to the lilies, I tell the little one, and learn
about the wild that's in them. Listen to it all,
they surprise us every year in places we
did not plant.

Look for freckles in mushrooms, but be careful
I warn the girl child. I tell her about strange things
and just a bit about fear. But most of all, I whisper,
love your Mother. She has come back to her mother
as you have come to her.
Baby girl and I watch a bird fly by
hoping we'll see it again.

My daughter has brought me her baby to love.

56

Blue flowers
on grandmother's
white china cup

By Marsha Mathews

*E*very morning while she reads the paper,
she drinks tea from a Lenox cup.
Then she dusts, sews,
embroiders tiny blue birds
into pillowcases,
frames flowered mountains
clipped from travel magazines.

Dinner's at 6:00 sharp.
If Granddad's not back
from golf on time,
she eats alone,
his pork chops biting
a cool white plate, blue-rimmed.

Every morning, she dresses the twins
Mother bore but couldn't raise,
prepares oatmeal and oranges.
As I leave for the school bus,
she listens to the Weather Channel.
If it rains, she puts on hose
and lipstick to drive me.

Onions and gravy shout dinner.
She pulls posts from the cabinets,
tap-taps a spoon.
The kettle whoos,
and the twins whoo with it.
Children eat first, napkins tucked.

Child at my Child

Mornings, she hangs diapers on the line,
repots an orchid,
nods to the neighbor,
sings Sinatra to her tomato plants.
An engine roars. She dashes to the front yard,
waves goodbye to Granddad.
Sometimes he sees her.

Dinner depends
on the success of Granddad's vending route,
the price of gas, the stocking of the food bank,
and on how much they had to send Mom
still finding herself in Idaho.

Grandfathers

By Paul Milenski

The two grandfathers love their first grandson, of course. The child is four, blonde, tousle-haired, brilliant, serious and sensitive. They know this child will be an artist and thus in need of their protection.

The child cries out in the night, "They are coming to get me. They are crossing the river. I can hear the tom-toms. I can see the canoes!" The child recalls a story of American Indians read to him by his mother. His imagination is vivid, in this case made terrifying because he has earaches: boom-boom-boom-boom, boom-boom-boom-boom, the throbbing like Indian war drums.

Szymon, his mother's father, is the grandfather who signs his name with X's. His is an illiterate's life of superstition, but also of native craftsmanship and wile. Apart from reading and writing, there is nothing that Szymon cannot do. He locates wild mushrooms in the woods, jigs up fish through the ice, uses basic tools skillfully to repair the irreparable. Szymon's is an ugly twisted lined face like the hag faces made from dried apples – on first appearance. On second, his is the most beautiful face in the world – wizened with man's basic goodness, with the merging of heart and soul.

The grandson kisses Symons' face, nuzzles with him as though he is nuzzling with his heart. Children are that wise.

"Chocz tutaj!" Syzmon says, a morning after one of his grandson's nights of terror. Szymon takes the child's little warm hand in his and the two walk down worn wooden stairs into the old basement to sit on little stools near an old wood pile.

"Oh pacz! Look at that!" Szymon pulls up a whittled stick of beech, applies his pocket knife to it in a final adjustment of form.

A dagger of wood, with hand and hilt glistening, the incuse whittles like little reverse fingernails, picking up gleams of light. The dagger looks formidable.

"Fee to dem Ind-i-ans!" Szymon says. He hands his grandson the wooden weapon and hugs him.

Out of the basement, the grandson waves the dagger at Pootsie. The hound whimpers and drags itself to safety under the kitchen table.

Zizz-zizz-zizz! The grandson makes swishing, cutting noises with the dagger. It is fearsome!

Szymon smiles with aged primitive humility and love

The second grandfather lives in the city. He speaks seven languages, listens to classical music, plays the cello, and has made a great success of himself. He too has heard of his first grandson's terrifying earaches, his nightmares and fearful screams in the dark.

"Come here, my blonde artist. How are you doing, son?"

This grandfather is Chester, tall, lean, distinguished looking. He wears a sport coat, shirt and tie, and cologne. His teeth, these generations old, are real and white and straight. He smiles, handsome as a movie star. His hair, once blonde is grey, but no less wavy and attractive.

Child at my Child

His is a big long hand on his grandson's back as the boy sits on his knee, "So, tell me about these Indians I hear so much about. What about these fellows? Have you thought they might just want to canoe across the river to make friends?"

"No."

"I see. Maybe they just want to picnic on your side of the river. They like where you live, I think."

"No!"

"Ah. They want to trade wampum and skins and artifacts for the things you have of value."

"I don't have value, grandpa."

"But you are most valued, my son." The big hand pulls the grandson closer for a warm hug.

The grandson throws his arms around his grandpa and hugs tightly. Umpf!

"You're very strong."

Umpf again.

"Very, Very! I like your pants and shirt. They're like mine with pockets. Do you have anything in the pockets?"

The grandson pulls out the pockets so they look like puppies' ears.

"Well, we can do something about that." This grandfather tucks the pants pocket in, drops in some Indian pennies, "Just in case they want to trade." Then he takes a Liberty Peace Dollar, holds it up to the sun until it gleams, "Have you ever seen silver so formidable?"

"No!"

"Hold it."

"Heavy, Grandpa."

I'm putting it here my son, into your shirt pocket. You're protected by the magic shield."

The two grandfathers visit the grandson as he sleeps in his bedroom. The child tosses and turns with the excitement of his imagination because his earaches have abated and the pain is less.

On his pillow are the dagger, the Indian pennies, and the silver dollar.

Hallowe'en

By Linda Lancione Moyer

Our tiny princess—prickly costume shed—
sits on Mom's lap in a pink sweatshirt, watching
Grandpa pushbroom the sidewalk under the laden persimmon.
"Hi, Nana," she fans me a wave. I drop a kiss
on her head, then pluck a low-hung hachiya,
and settle it into her hands. "Put it by Nana's purse,"
I say, reaching for more. She hesitates,
points to my black bag, "Eh?" Again, "Eh?"
gesturing at the fruit. Oh, purse/persimmon. To her,
they sound the same. It's a time of distinctions, between
toes and toast, Grandpa's cat Dusty and Nana's cat Duffy,
between the grandpa who comes every day and Papie,
who's arrived from afar and now emerges from the house,
face more veined than last year, scotch in hand.
Our son, right behind him sipping the same bitter gold,
sees the swept pile of squirrel-ravaged fruit
and goes for the ladder. In moments a full-blown harvest
is on, Grandpa reaching for the high ones, Papie and I
chaining the red-orange globes over to our granddaughter,
who bumps them into a paper bag with serious joy.
It's a mythic moment, generations harvesting in amber light.
Soon we'll help this girl sow her own backyard pumpkin,
learn snails and kales, sweet potatoes and potato bugs.
Later she'll glean a sense of single malt and sauvignon,
slowly make out for herself what nourishes, what poisons.

Child of my Child

Wordfalls

By Pearse Murray

ranny is leaving us, pet.
Why? *Because that is the way it is, love.*
Why? *Because all life must end.*
Why? *But you will see her again.*
My five-year-old-mind-asking whys.

Early evening light and darkening room,
with anxious air all 'round,
I am asked to leave the room.
I listen nearby for signs of something,
Pending something or other.

Something or other that says
something of Granny reading to me,
of the Cockatoo from Timbuktu
of Villains from Camillus
of the Yak from Iraq.

The look of words on her lips,
as she drenches me in her word spills
and reading my eyes as I read hers
understanding forever,
the whys of those who love
And the what I am from what I lost.

Child of my Child

The most
important thing
in the world

By Sheryl L. Nelms

*I*s my
four-month-old

twin grandson's thighbone
that was
broken
before
he was
born
then overlapped and fused
together
leaving it
thirty percent
shorter

than his
other

leg.

Child of my Child

Grandchild

By Karen Neuberg

We gather a child in our arms,
again. Patient in ways we were unable
to be for our own. Though those
days long and stretching were filled
with slow steps and explorations,
these seem profound. On the bus,
off the bus. Each day a candle
glowing in the sky, gathering time
in our pockets, falling through
holes in the seams. We gather
more: child of our child pronouncing
now our names, calling to us
across a room. Can anything be
more than this – or as simple.

Now
a mother
By Carol Nolde

*I*t's the way my daughter's arm encircles
her baby, whose bare back bends
toward the sand and waves that lap
at her mother's feet, her tiny
buttocks resting on the arm beneath her.

It's the way my daughter's body leans
toward the water, wanting the child to feel
the pull of sand and sea,
but only so much,
as someday she'll urge her
to greet an admiring stranger,
but hold her hand.

It's the way
their flesh meets
arm, buttocks, hand
the way I still long to touch the back
bent above the child,
want to hold them both,
knowing the bond that joins, separates.

Child of my Child

Natales

grate numeras?
Do you count your birthdays with gratitude?

By Charlotte Otten

*M*y granddaughter draws me, paints,
and cuts me out, a present for my birthday.
My legs, unevenly attached, dangle from
the refrigerator door

where she has pinned me,
held by magnets, left-overs from political
campaigns. Feet, cut off
and scotch-taped back onto my legs,

swing in opposite directions.
Is this how I will walk
not far from now? A large black ribbon
in my hair broods, a frontal omen.

Pupil-less blobs of blue stare
at me unseeing. I have no arms,
my body is as curveless as
the body of the 5-cent

celluloid doll
I had in the Depression
lipless, hairless,
no operating limbs.

But then I see: my paper-self's pink mouth
is stretched from ear to nonexistent ear,
and I smile back beyond the limits of my face,
glomming onto the image of unflagging love.

Child at my Child

False
teeth
By Barbara Redfield

everal years ago my 6 year old grandson, Willy, became fascinated by my new false teeth. He woke up early to make sure he did not miss the morning putting on of the glue. Yes, the red gooey stuff that dentures need to stay in place was the most amazing glue Willy had ever seen. At bedtime, he was not about to go to sleep, until he had personally put my teeth in the fizzy stuff for their over-night bath. When his cousin, Nicholas, came over for a play date, the first thing Willy wanted me to show him was how my teeth popped out!

I was trying to keep in mind some of the best advice I ever got from a group of guys at the Westchester Penitentiary where I did my initial training as a therapist. They loved that I came to work in my pearls and diamond stud earrings and did not try to dress down to artificially make myself look like one of them. They did not trust the Junior League Do-Gooders who volunteered at the Pen.

" You'en don't never be nothing you ain't! You be real cool, Barb'ra." So at age 66, I was trying to have fun with this new magic trick of mine. I was trying to be "cool" about my teeth, suddenly becoming a star attraction.

Shortly after my new teeth arrived, Willy took me to Grandparent Day at his school. As he was putting on his boots, at the end of the day, he slapped his head and said, "Oh, I forgot,
I wanted you to show my friends how your teeth come out." I calmly said. "We'll do it next time." A year later, I was babysitting for a week while Willy's parents were out of town. One morning at breakfast, he asked if I would come to school with him for show-and-tell and to show his friends my mysterious teeth. This kid never forgets a thing! This was NEXT TIME.
I said that I would talk to his teacher and ask her if it was okay.

As I explained to his teacher what Willy wanted me to do, I could sense some reluctance on her part. I heard my voice kick into a higher gear, trying to persuade her that I could do this in a gentle, non-threatening way, going so far as to recite my credentials as a therapist. She replied that she thought it would be a good idea to talk it over with the school nurse. You can guess the rest. Yes, the nurse thought it might be traumatic for some kids. I was worried about how to tell Willy I would not be able to come with my teeth act. His reaction, "oh, well, it's their sad". And, I, of course, agree.

I do not know whether my teeth can take full credit, but his cousin, Nicholas, can now put together a transformer action figure faster than the speed of lightening, without the use of red, goopy glue. I am, of course, the very first human he knew who was able to transform herself into an all new character in a matter of seconds. And, recently when Willy and I were hiking, I was out of breath, complaining about getting old and he without missing a beat said, " you're not old, you're real cool!" The guiding spirit of my old pals at the Pen is alive and well in Willy.

Poem for a granddaughter
who has carried the burden
of my name for a year

By Carlos Reyes

for Daphne Sloane Reyes Brandon

How can she know
    what the basket of our life contains?
    It should be a basket of flowers
    as it is springtime
    and given her first name . . .
    How can she know this name
    has anything to do with her?
    The name that doesn't seem to fit
    her family
    The name picked from the air
    even before her mother
    was born
    then given to her at birth,
    a whim let's say that now
    has become a tradition
    Well we are left with it
    a taken name
    for the centuries
    in future years
    Where did this name come from?
    How long will it last?
    We might as well ask
    where did we come from?
    How long will we last?
    Maybe in that far future
    any given surname
    will be only that
    a lovely label a name
    not something that sets
    people asking foolish questions
    about races, about background.

Child of my Child

The grandparents

By Larry Rubin

They were a pair of old Jews who hawked
And shriveled by the fire and forgot
The flame they had lost. They spoke a kind of language
I could never understand, and patted
My fat limbs and made me kiss them
Between the wrinkles. She fished up the nickels
From her moldy leather purse, and he
Turned the palsied pages of his book
And tried to show me how to read backwards.
It was a tricky business, and I gave up—
Too soon, though, because they died.
Now all her nickels rattle in my bones
And his parchments split in the cold room. And God
I try, but I cannot read those buried words.

Child of my Child

A nymph
for bruna
By Marion Brown St. Onge

As Bruna was skipping to school one day,
A nymph jumped from a tree.
With golden hair and French beret,
She was a sight to see!
Bruna, stunned, spoke not a word,
For she had never known
A nymph (a girl!) and quite like her,
An elfin flower-like clone.
The nymph said, Bru, I've come to surf
With you in Ha-wa-ii!
I've never been on earthly turf!
Oh! Come to the beach with me!
Behind the books in Bruna's pack
She kept her bi-ki-ni.
Her board was fastened to the back,
Her French beret aussi!
So off they went, a nymph and a girl,
Down to the sand and the sea.
And who in the world would catch that first curl?
But—our girl with a nymph on her knee!

Moral:
While as Bruna knows, You Don't Skip School!
I hope that you'll agree with me;
You'd be a fool to follow the rule,
When with a nymph you'd be free!

Ready
or not
By Natalie Safir

From the ante-room at St. Luke's Hospital, I could hear my daughter groaning. I was alert to every sound, waited for the characteristic cry of a newborn to split the fetid air. Remembering my own first birth experience, its endless development, kept me reasonably calm as the minutes labored by. Yet I was aware of my heart pounding unmercifully and a slow sweat leaking down under my shirt. Finally my son-in-law, all in white, blood smeared up the front of his hospital gown, came out with a look of bemused victory, puzzlement and relief.

"The baby's out," he said, "Whew, it's a boy. You can go in if you want."

Of course, I want, I thought, and entered the delivery room, which looked more like a battlefield. Nothing seemed in order, blood on sheets tangled and strewn about. Empty vials, used needles. The mess of it all struck me. How did I let all this go on without knowing exactly what was happening to her? How could I have left my child in their care? Did they know what they were doing? My daughter's face was pale and glistening with perspiration, her hair pasted to her head. Her eyes were teary. She had been hit by a truck and was still in a stupor from the blow.

My entire focus was on my daughter. This was what I knew, how to be a mother, nothing more. That there was a small, new life with us in the room, simply did not interest me. Only that she was all right, had survived the ordeal, would smile again.

I could not take my eyes from her.

"O my god, I did it," she said. "It was awful. But he's beautiful," she said, motioning to the bundle on the steel table the nurses were cleaning up. I glanced over, but felt only relief, no joy, resenting the prompt to release my gaze from my daughter's face.

"Don't you want to hold him, Ma?" she implored.

"Oh sure," I felt compelled to respond and opened my arms as the nurses placed the infant into them. This feeling, the lightweight, compact wrapped parcel was so strange; it had been twenty-four years. I looked at the infant, a fragile foreign wonder that had no relation to me. Looked into his dark little eyes.

Child of my Child

"Mom, you're a grandmother," she crooned, so pleased with herself and seeking my excitement. The best I could say was: "Isn't it wonderful," in a quiet, halting voice, while inside I was thinking, *No I'm not, I'm much too young; I'm not even married yet.* I was fifty, divorced from her father several years earlier.

My daughter had another son in the following four years. It had taken me so many years to organically grow into the role of grandmother. To feel that I could be the mother of a mother and to comprehend the meaning of this new life, how it extended and enriched mine. It was not a title I could print on a t-shirt or a flowery mug.

That little boy is about to graduate from college, his brother a senior in high school. Now the gift I want most from my other two daughters, aside from their happiness, is to be a Grandmother again.

A brief note
to Josephine,
from Diana

By Kenneth Salzmann

Take this quilt and let it blanket you,
in comfort and in loss.
It was stitched just for you
six generations ago.

Ever since, these colorful threads
have run through the lives
of daughters, then mothers,
then grandmothers, then daughters.

Take this quilt and one day
spread it over your own children
and over their children,
in comfort and in loss.

Everything is changing, and will.
But these ancient threads are holding fast.

Child of my Child

To a new
grandchild

By Mollie Schmidt

*Y*our name is Kristen, you are ten, but
I don't know you. When your mother
had you, no one told your father,
our youngest son.

                     Did he suspect
his brief affair had borne such fruit?
Did his instincts warn him – you're too
young for fatherhood?

                     Now, too late
to hold the baby in his arms in awe
at tiny fingers, nose, and mouth – but
soon enough to love, forgive, and

play the role our seed intended.

Child of my Child

Heirloom

By Ada Jill Schneider

This is the needle great-grandma held
to sew the buttons on the white silk blouse
grandma wore without asking first
that still has the stain that wouldn't wash out
from the chocolate bar that grandma ate
at the Paramount Theater with her date
while wearing the blouse that wasn't hers.

These are the spools of colorfast thread
great-grandma kept in her sewing chest
with remnants of garments and safety pins
in a jumble of rick-rack she bought to trim
grandma's wartime sailor dress
and ruffles that edged our kitchen shelves.

These are the quilts hand-stitched and stacked
pieced with the fabric of great-grandma's past
in a lavender-scented high-domed trunk
along with my poems which I have packed
for you to unfold for us to connect,
mutually linked like needles and thread.

Child of my Child

The art
of sitting
By Mary Kolada Scott

"*M*om, are you sitting down?" my son asked during a phone call. It was late at night, and this is never an auspicious opening line from a grown son who is a recovering drug addict. At least it wasn't another collect call from jail.

I *was* sitting down, but I wasn't prepared for what he said next.

"You're going to be a grandma," he said, and his whole life flashed before my eyes.

"But I just had *you*," I wailed. It seemed as though time had compressed and I was holding him for the first time. I hadn't known he was involved with anyone; he had casually mentioned seeing a girl only a week or two earlier.

The next months were filled with emotions. I met my son's baby's mama and her family. I retrieved my engagement ring and wedding band from the safe deposit box. My ex-husband had been dead for years, and I had promised my modest ring set to our son, whom we had adopted at birth.

There was an impromptu wedding ceremony at the courthouse so my son could move parole out of one county to live with his wife and her family in another jurisdiction. I wasn't invited to my only child's wedding.

An ultrasound showed a little girl. The bride was thrilled, but I cautioned her that ultrasounds weren't always accurate. She was not swayed and requested pink, frilly things for the baby shower and chose Kailey Nicole as the baby's name.

Another ultrasound just weeks before the birth revealed shocking news—a boy! There was a flurry of exchanging clothes and choosing a new name. God has a wicked sense of humor, I decided. ("She sure does," said a friend).

Jacob Brian was born last October. My son and his mother-in-law were in the delivery room while my husband and I waited outside. I am used to sitting. Mothers do a lot of sitting—at ballgames, doctors' offices, school open houses and Cub Scout meetings. Some of us sit in courtrooms and jail visiting rooms instead of on bleachers at graduations.

That morning, I sat waiting for my first grandchild. I represented my mother, who had died when my son was eight. I was a witness for my ex-husband, who would never know this child. I represented my son's birth mother, whose magnanimous gesture entitled me to sit here in her stead.

When my son held Jacob for the first time and raised him up to show me, I cried, remembering the first time I saw him through a nursery window. I was blessed once with a baby I never imagined I could have and now with a grandchild I had never envisioned in my life.

Jacob was perfect and as beautiful as his father had been. I held him and he sneezed for the first time. Already he was reacting to the world around him, one in which I would orbit his tiny existence.

A modern mother, I know too well this scenario still carries potential for heartbreak. Drugs, divorce or distance could separate us. I don't have much experience as a grandmother. I don't have words of wisdom or extravagant expectations.

But for now I am a typical grandma. I fuss over Jacob and delight in every ordinary movement and expression. I coax smiles and inhale his new-baby smell. I buy clothes I wish I could have afforded for my own son. I collect books to read to Jacob as I had to his father. I show his photographs to everyone.

Mostly, I just hold my grandbaby. And sit.

Jonathan
loves loons

By Joanne Seltzer

He loves to hear their soul-
   piercing calls
   across Lake Winnipesaukee.

He loves to watch them swim
along the shore,
then dive and disappear.

He loves the loon store we visit,
the loon book I bought him.
He doesn't love the motorboats
that menace fragile nests.

I'm Jonathan's grandmother.
He loves loons more than ducks,
more than Canadian geese
but less than I love Jonathan.

Towers:
Century City, LA
By Myra Shapiro

On a crescent-curved balcony, 15 floors above
the Avenue of the Stars,
6 lanes of multi-colored metal traffic zipping back and forth,
in the middle a strip designed
not only to divide cars North and South but to entertain the traveler,
its eye of concrete,
grass and lily-shaped spigots projecting water skyward, cadenced

shush, shush, shush rocketing
over the rumble of motors, I am waiting for a birth, the birth of
our first grandchild,
the third generation conceived in this new world where—imagine it!—
the grandchild of a Rabbi
meets a Pakistani Muslim, they fall in love no matter what
we fear, and they will
have a baby whose name will be as old as

history. Benjamin.
And I will plant a garden with flowers for his eyes
because I will not be here,
because I want to give him a ground of many colors: coreopsis,
black-eyed Susans, my father's dahlias,
Mama's herbs—seeds that can be lifted by the wind or beaks of birds
flying over time zones, oceans.

Last night I dreamed I watched for hours a baby's babbling
and twisting, babbling
and shifting, when suddenly he spoke—"Bon, bon," and then
"Good, good"—two languages!—
heavenly labials in a world of gutturals. In this city of the angels
which may fall at any moment,
I take as blessing the two-ness of his speech, believing
generosity will save him.

Age is heavy
on the ground

By Johnmichael Simon

*A*ge is heavy on the ground
  alongside the pansies and begonia
  the fuchsia and snapdragons
  the tulips, the pomegranates
  just beginning to swell
  the pomelo now into its second month
  fragrant; trowel and fork
  watering can sprinkling, she stoops

Age is heavy on the ground
between the roses and the bougainvillea
in loose balloon-cloth-yellow shorts
down to her knees she bends
pulls at a weed, age is broad and heavy
her red tee shirt flaps pendulous as the wind

Yesterday's windfalls are on the ground
she gathers peaches, ripe and rescued
from ants and birds, soon she will wash
cut up, make some jam, tonight the grandchildren
will be coming, there will be chicken
honeyed, crisp and herbed, potatoes from
the garden sprinkled with parsley
grape juice with a splash of club soda
bread rolls from her own grandmother's recipe

But first there are some poems to be typed
the ones about the sounds at dawn, the wind,
the lost kitten she'd rescued, the concerto
of Saint-Saens, her notes on the latest novel
for the book club

Soon the grandchildren will arrive.
She sets the table, answers the phone, arranges
flowers in vases, puts on some nice music,
showers, dresses, perhaps a drop of perfume
a stick of incense perhaps in the bathroom?
The papers, the emails, turn down the flame
under the soup

Age is heavy on the ground
from flower to fruit
to candle glow on silverware and china

Age is heavy on the ground
weightless as a butterfly

Child of my Child

Tesla Rose,
3 weeks

By John Oliver Simon

*Y*our blue eyes track our faces now,
the sunny constellation of your mommy,
Daddy's high-striding, mountain range,
and this snow-bearded person who looms
into view, a good heart, you've decided,
to go to sleep on, enclosing your inner
sensorium in dreams of sucking.

Born a century to within five weeks
after your great-grandma who smoked
like a chimney and sat on the egg of
her secret fifty years, you stretch fingers
toward understanding your own name,
your neurons dividing and redividing,
copper wire sparking, petals slowly unfold.

Tesla Rose,
14 ½ months

By John Oliver Simon

*N*ow you're a big girl and you walk by yourself,
I spot you up the steps of the dark tower.
Up there, on the battlements, in the kitchen,
two witches, five or six, are making dinner
out of sand. Their names are Gretchen and Isis,
they know the secret language of fantasy.
Isis takes our order on an action figure:
Chow Mein. Gretchen fills a blue bowl up with sand.
You empty sand on the deck and mouth the bowl.
Gretchen doesn't understand the word agua.
What little water's left was carried for miles
in my pocket, as you slept against my chest
in the May sun, past all your grandmothers' doors.

Child at my Child

Apricots
for Isaac

By Elaine Starkman

The sky was a clear jewel.
My grandson and I roamed
an open orchard, one of the last.

A space between the park
and my house. He was a spy walking,
wandering the worn path, not the new one.

He had just begun to worry about foxtails
sticking in his socks when he saw apricot trees
hung with fruit, not yet ripe,

but small globes of gold and orange.
He gave me his spy cap and climbed up.
"Here, Grandma," he called,

throwing fruit down to me
with a child's delight I'd forgotten,
21st century Tom Sawyer, red hair and freckles.

In the abandoned orchard
picking apricots and chasing off ants
I remembered lost worlds:

I hadn't seen fruit-bearing trees
until I was twenty and by thirty
I had no time to savor them.
Only now do I know
what I'd mistaken for wisdom.

Child of my Child

My Thirteen
year old grandson
By Parker Towle

We paced down
Huntington Avenue
beside the Science dome
of Christendom and its
mirror pool headed for
Symphony Hall, Boston.
His huge
leather shoes agitated
the sidewalk in acute
distress. An alien
from some distant planet
hummed beneath his baggy pants,
themselves obscured
by shirttails striving
to live
free, flapping beneath
a jacket. Yes, he was clearly
an emissary from some
galaxy spinning far away. At last
in the crowd waiting to cross
the avenue the streaming tails
were gathered loosely
under
his belt. We entered, rose
the stairs and sauntered down
the corridor outside the hall,
by the gallery of players and
a hundred years of maestros,
through the dowagers
of a Friday afternoon,
the lame,

Child of my Child

the furred, the regal gray.
Classic composers' busts
from above the balcony
glared down on us
with marble stares. Players
sifted in. Maestro followed
weaving through chairs.
            They played
with other worldly
beauty. For finale Elgar
soared on the lips of risen
brass. The lad and all the audience
surged in a maelstrom of applause.
The shirttails did not
                    escape.
He ran from the hall as if
in panic to release his feet
and the belted tails from their
cruel bondage. At the car,
the music still swirling,
in tee shirt and sneaks he reentered
the feel of his natural world.

On becoming
a grandmother

By Karen Waggoner

"You know, I always did think that girl had a great set," our friend stage-whispered to my husband under the clatter of plates being stacked after dinner. I pretended I didn't hear just as I usually did in my classroom when I chose not to get involved.

My husband glanced across the table at our daughter-in-law, a beautiful and bountiful brunette. "Yeah," he muttered, "I think this is gonna be good for her." He smiled indulgently at his friend. "She says she's already gained about ten pounds." Once again, I could hear him, but kept my face turned away while I pretended to listen to another conversation. I was offended by the two men discussing our son's wife and her attributes as if she were not in the room. There was more to my annoyance, but I continued to ignore both the remarks and my own reaction.

The hostess's mother-in-law was the only person at the table not familiar to the rest of us, but even she began to nod and smile knowingly as my husband and his buddy elbowed each other and winked as if they were still nine years old. Even more annoyed, I assisted our hostess who was clearing the table, her face impassive, apparently uninvolved with the rude men. I carried the turkey platter to the kitchen, hoping to stay away from the dining room.

Later I sat at the kitchen table with my friend, her daughter, and her mother, perusing a fashion catalog while the rest of the crowd watched a football game in the family room. I temporarily forgot my irritation with the men; their voices had become a murmur. Suddenly my husband appeared at my side, grinning. He announced in a very loud voice, "Will all those not going to be a grandmother stand up?" My friend's mother pushed back her chair and stood. Then the daughter did the same. At last my friend rose to join the crowd standing around the table staring at me. I was the only one seated.

It's still peculiar and humiliating to me that I had such a reaction to the news of impending grandmotherhood. I always wanted my son and his wife to have children, but I thought they weren't ready. More likely, I wasn't ready. I was mortified that I had ignored all the signals flying around the dinner table. Despite quite a lot of effort, I could find no explanation except to state over and over, "But I'm only 48 years old. That's too young." I knew instantly that my statement was both stupid and hurtful to the young couple. After all, the reason I thought I was young to be a grandmother was because I gave birth to my son when I was only 22. He and his wife were mature enough to have children, and they certainly did not need my permission.

In hindsight I'm grateful that I found the right apology for my behavior, and that I managed to be enthusiastic long before the baby arrived. The granddaughter's existence has been a blessing, culminating with attending her university graduation last year. I'm counting on being around for more milestones in her life, possibly being a great grandmother too. But now that I'm past 70 and have two new baby grandchildren, I can't help thinking it would be great if I were still 48. I'll be lucky to see them graduate from high school.

Before my
grandson's surgery

By Donna Wahlert

A thousand miles away from you
I do not know where to turn.
I visit the Trappestine Monastery,
then sit on a bench by their small lake.
I read, I pray, I contemplate.

An anhinga hangs from a fallen tree
drying out like a sail in the wind.
A snakebird darts under
the water like a crafty fish;
a salamander separates from his tail,
then scampers away.

Thoughts of you beat in me
like the snowy egret's wings.
I think of your tiny body,
that mite of kidney,
that thread of tubing tangled
like knitting yarn.

These minutes, these hours, hang
like that still anhinga. I want to dive
with you into the smooth cool lake.
I want us to separate from the pain
like the salamander. I want to run
with you to a safer place.

Just when I thought I was too old to fall in love again,
I became a grandparent.

–Author Unknown

Join the Conversation . . .
If you . . . are . . . have . . . or love. . . a grandparent,
Please visit us online at www.ChildOfMyChild.biz
To share your own stories and experiences.

Child of my Child

ABOUT THE CONTRIBUTORS

Barbara Adams has published two books of poetry, <u>Hapax Legomena</u> and <u>The Ordinary Living</u> and a book of literary criticism, The Enemy Self: Poetry and Criticism of Laura Riding. Her poems, stories and essays have been published in literary and professional journals, including *The Nation, Texas Review, Negative Capability, Confrontation, Modern Poetry Studies, Psychoanalytic Review, Home Planet New.* She has been anthologized in *Riverine* and *WaterWrites. In 2007,* she won the Robert Frost Foundation Award for her poem *"Henry Jones, from Wales."* Her story, *"Portrait of the Artist's Daughter,"* won first prize in the 1999 Negative Capability Fiction Contest. Her one-act play, <u>God's Lioness & the Crow: Sylvia Plath & Ted Hughes</u>, was produced by Mohonk Mountain Stage Company in New Paltz, New York in 2000.

Christine Allen-Yazzie's novel, <u>The Arc and the Sediment</u>, won an IPPY Award, the Utah Book Award, as well as best novel and best book-length work from the Utah Arts Council. The story was a finalist for the James Jones First Novel Competition. Her fiction and poetry have been published in numerous literary journals. She lives in Utah, where she teaches writing at the University of Utah.

Diana M. Amadeo has been published in 500 publications, including books, anthologies, magazines, newspapers and online. She won the 2006 Catholic Press Association Book Award and the 2009 Angel Animal Network Story Award.

Lynore Banchhoff's work has appeared in such publications as *Friends Journal, Juggler's World, Knowing Stones: Poems of Exotic Places.* In 2009, she published the chapbook, <u>Past Tense and Parts of Speech on Beech Street</u>.

Helen Bar-Lev is Senior Editor of *Cyclamens and Swords Publishing* (www.cyclamensandswords.com), former Editor-in-Chief of <u>Voices: Israel Annual Anthology</u>, Poetry Editor for *Presence: An International Journal of Spiritual Direction*, published by Spiritual Directors International www.sdiworld.org and a contributing editor for Sketchbook: *A Journal for Eastern and Western Short Form* (http://poetrywriting.org/). She lives in Israel

Drama, fiction, and poetry by **K. Biadaszkiewicz** has been produced and/or published in North America, Europe, and Asia. <u>Her play, He Came Home One Day While I Was Washing Dishes</u>, is included in the Applause Books anthology, <u>Best American Short Plays</u> (2005).

Regina Murray Brault has twice been nominated for the Pushcart Prize, and her poetry has appeared in approximately 95 different publications, including: *Ancient Paths Literary Magazine, Comstock Review, Grandmother Earth, Hartford Courant,* Anthology of New England Writers, Mothers and Daughters (Ed. June Cotner 1999), *Karamu, Mennonite, Northwoods Journal, Poet Magazine, and State Street Review.* She is also the recipient of more than 240 poetry awards including first place in the 2007 Euphoria Poetry Competition, the Skysaje Enterprises 2007 Poetry Competition, and the 2008 Creekwalker Poetry Award.

Clinton B. Campbell's work has appeared in periodicals and anthologies including *Margie, California Quarterly, Passager, Writer's Digest and Journal of NJ Poets. His poem, "Club Soda Nights,"* was published in After Shocks: The Poetry of Recovery for Life-Shattering Events. His work also appears in *The Cancer Poetry Project, and his poem, "My Veteran's Day Prayer,"* was entered into the Congressional Record by Congressman Joe Wilson on 11/9/07. He lives in Beaufort, South Carolina with his wife, photographer/poet Karen M. Peluso.

Sherry Gage Chappelle of Rehoboth Beach, Delaware, has been awarded two grants by the Delaware Division of the Arts and has been chosen for two of the state's Poet Laureate retreats. Her collection Moving Forward, Looking Back was runner up for the 2009 Dogfish Head Poetry Prize. Her grandchildren, a son and daughter of her stepson's, and her son's twin boys, are endless sources of amusement and amazement and a fine writing resource.

Elayne Clift lives in Saxtons River, Vermont. Her latest book is ACHAN: A Year of Teaching in Thailand (Bangkok Books, 2007). She has just completed her first novel, Hester's Daughters, based on Nathaniel Hawthorne's The Scarlet Letter. Her granddaughter's "other" grandma lives in Bangladesh.

Edward M. Cohen's novel, $250,000 was published by Putnam's. His non-fiction books have been published by Prentice-Hall, Prima, SUNY Press, Limelight. Over 30 of his stories have appeared in literary journals and anthologies. His articles and essays have appeared in *Cosmopolitan, Child, Parenting, American Woman, Jewish Arts Festival of Life Guide and Library Journal.* His work has won awards in the Loren Hemingway story contest, Bruce Brown Foundation short fiction contest and the Evergreen Chronicles Novella Contests. He has been a four-time fellow at the Edward Albee foundation and recipient of the John Golden Award and grants from the National Endowment for the Arts and New York State Council on the Arts.

Child of my Child

Barbara Crooker has published poems in magazines such as *The Hollins Critic, The Beloit Poetry Journal, America, The Atlanta Review, The Green Mountains Review, and The Denver Quarterly.* She is anthologized in such works as *The Bedford Introduction* to <u>Literature and The Bedford Introduction to Poetry ,</u> <u>Worlds in Our Words: Contemporary American Women Writers</u> (Prentice Hall), <u>Whatever It Takes: Women Writing on Women's Sports</u> (Farrar, Straus & Giroux). Also the poet has written ten chapbooks, and three full-length books: <u>Radiance</u>, which won the 2005 Word Press First Book Award and was a finalist for the 2006 Paterson Poetry Prize; <u>Line Dance</u> (Word Press, 2008), which won the 2009 Paterson Prize for Literary Excellence; and <u>More</u>, which is forthcoming from C&R Press in 2010. She has received three Pennsylvania Council on the Arts Fellowships in Literature, and won these national poetry competitions: the 1997 *Karamu* Poetry Prize, the New Millennium Writings Y2K Award, the 2001 ByLine Chapbook Competition, the 2003 Thomas Merton Poetry of the Sacred Award, the 2004 WB Yeats Society of NY Poetry Prize, the 2004 Grayson Books Chapbook Competition, The 2006 *Rosebud* Ekphrastic Poetry Prize, and 2007 the <u>Anthology Of New England Writers</u> Pen and Brush Poetry Prize. Garrison Keillor has read eighteen of her poems on "The Writer's Almanac."

Darcy Cummings has received awards and fellowships from Yaddo, Virginia Center for the Creative Arts, and the Dodge Foundation. Her book of poems, <u>The Artist As Alice: From A Photographer's Life</u>, won the Bright Hills Press Award and was published in 2006.

Laurie Lee Didesch's poetry has appeared or is forthcoming in *The Comstock Review, The Macguffin, Karamu, White Pelican Review, California Quarterly, Artisan: A Journal Of Craft, The Awakenings Review, Feast Of Fools: Poems, Stories, and Essays On Sacred Fools, Tricksters and others.* She has also won several awards, including First Place in the Sinipee Writers' Annual Poetry Contest.

Meredith Escudier has published essays, poetry and memoir in numerous literary journals and magazines. Her work has appeared or is forthcoming in such publications as *Pharos, Upstairs at Duroc,* www.alimentumjournal. com, www.culinate.com , www.imitationfruit.com, www.newversenews.com; anthologies including *Steeped in the World of Tea, Let Them Eat Crêpes and the International Herald Tribune.* She also writes a lighthearted monthly column on language at www.blablablah.org, She is a native Californian and a longtime resident of France.

Michael Estabrook is a poet who lives in Massachusetts with his wife (and high school sweetheart) Patti. They have been blessed with three children and thus far three grandchildren.

Barbara V. Evers is an active member of South Carolina Writers' Workshop and serves as the Past President Ex Officio of the Board of Directors. One of her short stories was published in *Variety*.

Anne C. Fowler is the author of five poetry chapbooks: <u>Five Islands, Whiskey Stitching, Summer of Salvage</u>, and <u>What I Could</u>, all published by Pudding House Press and <u>Liz, Wear Those Pearl Earrings</u>, winner of the Frank Cat Press 2002 Chapbook Contest. She is an Episcopal priest and rector of St. John's Church in Jamaica Plain, Massachusetts, and for ten years she ran the Chapter & Verse Reading Series in her home town.

Hugh Fox has been a leading figure in contemporary poetry and literary publishing for decades. He is the author of 110 books, primarily poetry, and the recipient of numerous awards and honors, including a Fulbright professorship. His most recent book is <u>The Collected Poetry of Hugh Fox</u> (World Audience).

Lewis Gardner's poems have appeared in a number of anthologies and other publications, including more than 60 of his poems and light verse pieces in the pages of the *New York Times*. A staged version of his poetry collection Tales of the Middlesex Canal, which was originally performed at New York City's Greenwich House Theater by a cast led by Academy Award-winning actor Kim Hunter, has been presented in several locations in upstate New York and Massachusetts. Twice a finalist for the Walt Whitman Award, he is coauthor of the book <u>Children of the Wild</u>, a study of feral children. His play "<u>Pete & Joe at the Dew Drop Inn</u>" will appear in the forthcoming <u>Best American Short Plays 2008-2009</u>. He has taught writing workshops for New York University and the New Jersey State Council on the Arts Poets in the Schools program.

Sandi Gelles-Cole is an editor in the book publishing business since 1973, working initially for major conventional publishers and in 1983 launching Gelles-Cole Literary Enterprises, her own editorial boutique. She and her husband, Kenneth Salzmann, initiated CHILD OF MY CHILD to celebrate the birth of Josephine Salzmann. She is currently working on a novel to be published next spring by Gelles-Cole Literary Enterprises.

Carol Gordon's writing has been published in *Calyx, Bellingham Review, Poetry Seattle, Kalliope*, and others. My chapbook, Lost Stone, was published by Flume Press. She describes herself as "a life-long West-Coaster."

John Grey has published extensively in literary journals, magazines and anthologies. His work was recently published in *Connecticut Review, Kestrel and Writer's Bloc*. He has poems forthcoming in *Pennsylvania English, Alimentum and the Great American Poetry Show*. Mr. Grey is an Australian-born poet who has lived in the U.S. for more than thirty years. He notes that he is not a grandparent himself, but his contribution to Child of My Child was "inspired by my mother and her ever-expanding brood."

Nancy Gustafson has published poetry, short fiction and articles in anthologies and journals, including Angel Face (MaryAnka Press), Beautiful Women: Like You and Me (Baxter Press), A Cup of Comfort for Weddings (Adams Media), Poems of Ghosts, Evil and Superstition (Level 4 Press), Modern Nursery Rhymes (Level 4 Press), Poems of Inspiration and Faith (Level 4 Press), Mom Writing Literary Magazine, Tree Magic: Nature's Antennas (SunShine Press Publications), Gardening At A Deeper Level (Garden House Press), Rocking Chair Reader: Coming Home (Adams Media Corporation), A Cup of Comfort for Inspiration (Adams Media Corporation), Suddenly IV and Suddenly V (Stone River Press), *Lucidity Poetry Journal, The Herbalist's Journal* (Ft. Worth garden society), *The MAADvocate, Banshee Studios Magazine* (e-zine: bansheestudios. net), and Poetry Society of Texas Book of the Year. She lives with her husband, Jan, in Huntsville, Texas.

Werner Hengst has written more than fifty essays dealing with nature, travel, adventure and with growing up in wartime Germany. His work has been published in *Smithsonian, Snowy Egret* and in several anthologies and newspapers. He lives in Somers, NY with his wife Betty.

Barbara Hoffman was a first runner-up for 2008 Bordighera Poetry Prize for her chapbook, Lilacs From the Truck. She is the subject of the WLIW Channel 21 show "Originals: Arts on Long Island" series.

Louise Jaffe has published four poetry chapbooks and a collection of three novellas about female empowerment. She has had poems published in a wide variety of anthologies including <u>Voices of Brooklyn, Sarah's Daughters Sing, Which Lillith and The Great American Poetry Show</u>. Also Ms. Jaffe's work has appeared in literary journals including *Lambs and Trochees, Slant, The Jewish Women's Literary Annual, Espirit, Mid-America Poetry Review, Buckle & and Calliope.*

David James' latest book, <u>She Dances Like Mussolini</u>, was published in 2009. His one-act plays have been produced in California, Massachusetts, Michigan, and New York.

Sheila Golburgh Johnson is a former student of the late British poet laureate Ted Hughes. Her poems have appeared in literary magazines such as *Poetry East, Blue Mesa Review, Connecticut Review, and Jewish Women's Literary Annual.* She has is a recipient of the Writer's Digest Award, the Chester Jones Award, and the Sydney Taylor Award for her novel, <u>After I Said No</u>. In 1999, Sheila won the international Reuben Rose Award for Poetry, and was invited to read at the International Forum for Literature and Culture in Haifa, Israel, where she shared her work with Egyptian, Palestinian, Korean, Israeli, Mexican, and Finnish poets.

Pearl Karrer is an editor for the *California Quarterly*, a poetry journal entering its 38th year. Her poetry has been recognized in *The MacGuffin's* National Poet Hunt 2002 and 2007 and in the Arts Council Silicon Valley's *A Poem a Day* contest for April, 2010. Her poetry has appeared in numerous publications, including *Artword Quarterly, Bayou, Berkeley Poetry Review, Black Buzzard Review, Buckle &, The Burning Cloud Review, California Quarterly, Cider Press Review, Clackamas Literary Review, Concrete Wolf, Coffee & Chicory, The Devil's Millhopper, Dexter Review, The Dickinson Review, Gaia, Green Fuse, Ibis, International Poetry Review, Into The Teeth Of The Wind, The Jabberwock Review, Karamu, languageandculture.net, Liberty Hill Poetry Review, The Lucid Stone, The MacGuffin, Manzanita, New Voices In Poetry and Prose, Northern Contours, Outdoor California, Pacific Coast Journal, Poets On:, Red Owl, Red Wheelbarrow, Runes, Slant, Steam Ticket, Sunrust, Visions-International, Whetstone, White Pelican Review*, and nine anthologies including the Chester H. Jones Foundation's <u>National Poetry Competition Winners 1989 and 2000</u>. She has two chapbooks: <u>Weathering</u> (Slapering Hol Press), <u>The Thorn Fence</u> (Finishing Line Press).

Charlene Langfur has published in *The Adirondack Review, Poetry East, Literal Latte,* among others. Her recent work appears in *Blueline, Green Mountains Review, and Room*, and in the anthology <u>Beloved on the Earth: 150 Poems of Grief and Gratitude</u> (Holy Cow! Press).

Janet M. Lewis has published two books of poetry, <u>Poems from Merrie Lane, and Getting Kind of Late</u>. Some of her poems have appeared in six different issues of *Manorborn*. She has also been published in *The Harford Poet*, one in *Poet's Ink*, and in *The Gunpowder Review, 2009. She won second prize in* a Walrus Press contest, and an honorable mention from the Oregon State Poetry Association. Two of her poems appeared in the Literary Journal Sundry. Her work has appeared in the anthology, <u>Migrants & Stowaways</u>, (Knoxville Writers' Guild, 2004).

Naomi Ruth Lowinsky's poems have appeared in *Left Curve, Bogg, Ibbetson Street Press, New Millennium Writings, The Pinch, Poem, Quiddity, The Spoon River Poetry Review and Westview.* She is the author of a memoir, <u>The *Sister from Below: When the Muse Gets Her Way*</u>. Her poem *"Madelyn Dunham, Passing On"* won first prize in the Obama Millennium Contest. Her third poetry collection, <u>*Adagio and Lamentation*</u>, was published in the summer of 2010. She is a Jungian analyst in private practice in Berkeley, CA and the poetry editor of Psychological Perspectives, published by the Los Angeles Jung Institute.

Mary Makofske's poems have appeared in Poetry, Zone 3, *Poetry East, Natural Bridge, Calyx, Amoskeag, Mississippi Review*, and other magazines and in the anthologies In a <u>Fine Frenzy: Poets Respond to Shakespeare</u> (Iowa) and <u>Hunger and Thirst</u> (San Diego City Works). She is the author of <u>The Disappearance of Gargoyles</u> (Thorntree) and <u>Eating Nasturtiums</u>, winner of a Flume Press chapbook competition.

Arlene Mandell, a former writer/editor at *Good Housekeeping Magazine*, has published poetry in 16 anthologies and more than 350 publications, including *Brevities, The New York Times, and Tiny Lights*. Her latest work is <u>Scenes from My Life on Hemlock Street: A Brooklyn Memoir</u>. She lives in Santa Rosa, CA. Ms. Mandell reports that "Breaking the Code" was written in 1995 when her first and only grandchild was 2 1/2 years old.

Rochelle Mass, is a translator and editor (*Kibbutz Trends*, bi-annual of cultural/political issues).She has published two poetry collections, <u>Aftertaste</u>,(Ride the Wind Press, Canada), as well as a smaller chapbook called, <u>Where's my Home</u> published by the Premier Poets Series in Rhode Island. A short story of hers was nominated for the 2002 Pushcart Prize by *The Paumanok Review* and short-listed for a Radio Play by the BBCMs Mass lives in Israel.

Marsha Mathews, a poet and novelist, is the author of <u>Northbound Single-Lane</u> (Finishing Line Press). She is an Associate Professor of English at Dalton State College in Dalton, Georgia.

Paul Milenski has won four consecutive PEN Syndicated Fiction Awards, an AWP International Prize for the Short-short, a Millennium prize for creative non-fiction, and has been runner up twice each in both Capricorn and Bobst Fiction Competitions. His Short-short, "Tickits," was made into an award winning art film by Universal Studios and Upstart Productions. He lives in Dalton, Massachusetts.

Linda Lancione Moyer has been published in *Atlanta Review, Cimarron Review, Connecticut Review, Compass Rose, CrazyHorse, Eclipse, Jabberwock The MacGuffin, Notre Dame Review, Poet Lore, and Post Road*, among other literary journals. Her most recent chapbook is <u>2% Organic, 32 Short Poems from a West Marin Dairy Barn</u>, In 2008 she was a resident at the Helene Wurlitzer Foundation in Taos, New Mexico. She lives in Berkeley, California.

Pearse Murray has a number of poems published in anthologies such as; <u>Tree Magic, Voices Israel, Miriam Lindbergh Poems for Peace 2002, 2004, Mizmour, L'David, Volume 1: The Shoah</u>, Also Mr. Murray's poems appear on line journals *Poetica Magazine and Cyclamens & Swords*. He lives in Albany, New York.

Sheryl L. Nelms' work has been published in such magazines, anthologies and textbooks as *Readers Digest, Modern Maturity, Kaleidoscope, Capper's, Grit, Country Woman, Poetry Now, Confrontation*, Strings, This <u>Delicious Day, The American Anthology and Men Freeing Men</u>. Fourteen collections of her poetry have been published.

Karen Neuberg's chapbook, <u>Detailed Still</u>, is available from Poets Wear Prada Press (2009). Her poems have appeared in *Barrow Street, Boxcar Poetry Review, Diagram, Free Verse, Mannequin Envy, and the anthology, Riverine: An Anthology of Hudson Valley Writers*, among others. She is a Pushcart and Best of the Net nominee and is associate editor of *Inertia Magazine*.

Carole Nolde has been published in such publications as *Hellas, The MacGuffin, The Comstock Review, Adirondac, Ekphrasis, Whetstone and The California State Poetry Quarterly*. Her poetry was recently anthologized in *Knowing Stones: Poems of Exotic Places* and the second edition of *Love is Ageless—Stories About Alzheimer's Disease.*

Charlotte F. Otten is the editor of The Book of Birth Poetry (Virago/Bantam) and Of English Women's Voices 1540-1700 (University of Florida Press). Her picture book, January Rides The Wind: A Book of Months was selected as a Book of the Year by the Bank Street College of Education and by *Booklist*. Her work of historical fiction for Intermediate Readers, Home In A Wilderness Fort: Copper Harbor 1844 was nominated for a Notable Michigan of the Year. Her poems have appeared in many journals, including *The Christian Science Monitor, Poems From Aberystwyth, And The Healing Muse.*

Barbara S. Redfield is a granddaughter, great-granddaughter and grandmother to generations of trout fishers, along with her career as an artist, writer and teacher.

Carlos Reyes has most recently published The Book of Shadows; New and Selected Poems (2009). Other recent books: At the Edge of the Western Wave (2004) A Suitcase Full of Crows a Bluestem Prize winner and finalist for 1996 Oregon Book Awards. Reyes' translation of the *Obra poética completa* (Complete Poetic Works) of Ecuadorean poet Jorge Carrera Andrade was published in 2004 in a bilingual edition in Ecuador. He is the publisher/editor of Trask House Books, Inc. In 2007 he was awarded a Heinrich Boll Fellowship to write on Achill Island, Ireland and in 2008 was awarded the Ethel Fortnter Award from St Andrews College. He was recently the poet-in-Residence in the Joshua Tree National Park.

Larry Rubin has published four books of poems, most recently Unanswered Calls (Kendall/Hunt, 1999) and received two annual awards from the Poetry Society of America (in 1961 and 1972) He has been published in *The New Yorker and Harper's Magazine* as well as the literary journal *Sewanee Review*. His work has been anthologized in The Norton Introduction to Literature (several editions) and A Geography of Poets (Bantam, 1979).

Natalie Safir is the author of five collections of poetry, critical reviews, essays and an adult fairy tale. Her poem "Matisse's Dance" is annually anthologized in college texts by The McGraw Hill Co. She has three grown daughters, enjoys two grandsons and two step-grandsons. She lives along the Hudson River, returning to Tarrytown where she teaches at The Neighborhood House and The Hudson Valley Writers' Center.

Marian Brown St. Onge has published travelers' guides, articles on twentieth century women writers, cultural issues and topics in international education. Beyond her poems—15 published so far—she is working on a biography of a French Word War II Resistance leader and poet—for which she received a Norman Mailer Fellowship award in summer 2009.

Kenneth Salzmann has been active in literary publishing and programming for more than thirty years. His poetry has appeared in such journals as *Rattle, Comstock Review, Sow's Ear Poetry Journal, Memoir (and)*, and in anthologies including <u>Beloved on the Earth: 150 Poems of Grief and Gratitude</u> (Holy Cow! Press), <u>Riverine: An Anthology of Hudson Valley Writers</u> (Codhill Press), and the forthcoming <u>Obamamentum</u> (Ohio Univ. Press/Ayebia).

Mollie Schmidt has published a children's book, <u>Willem of Holland</u>, 2008, as well as poems, reviews, and professional articles. She lives on a lake in central Maine, where nine grandchildren frequently visit.

Ada Jill Schneider, winner of the National Galway Kinnell Poetry Prize, is the author of several volumes of poetry, most recently <u>Behind the Pictures I Hang</u>, published by Spinner Publications in 2007. She directs "The Pleasure of Poetry," a program she founded, at the Somerset Public Library in Massachusetts and reviews poetry books for *Midstream magazine*.

Mary Kolada Scott has been published in numerous periodicals, journals and poetry collections. Recent publications include a poem in <u>Her Mark 2010</u> (Woman Made Gallery, Chicago) and two poems in the Summer 2009 issue of Calyx. Another poem appears in <u>When Last on the Mountain: The View from Writers over Fifty</u> (Holy Cow! Press). She became a grandmother in October 2009. She lives in Ventura, California, with her husband, Don.

Joanne Seltzer's poems have appeared in many literary journals and anthologies, including *The Village Voice, The Minnesota Review, and When I Am an Old Woman I Shall Wear Purple.* Her newest poetry collection, <u>Women Born During Tornadoes</u>, is published by Plain View Press. Seltzer's poem, "I Sing the Shekhinah's Praise," was chosen as a runner-up in the most recent Charlotte Newberger Poetry Competition and will be published in a forthcoming issue of *Lilith*, a Jewish feminist magazine.

Myra Shapiro's poems have appeared in many periodicals and in anthologies such as <u>The Best American Poetry (1999 and 2003)</u>. She is the recipient of The Dylan Thomas Poetry Award from The New School and was the finalist for The Robert H. Winner Prize from the Poetry Society of America. Her book of poems, <u>I'll See You Thursday</u>, was published by Blue Sofa Press in 1996. In 2007 Chicory Blue Press published her memoir, <u>Four Sublets: Becoming a Poet in New York.</u>

Johnmichael Simon has published three books of poems and two collaborations with partner Helen Bar-Lev. His poetry has been awarded numerous prizes and honorable mentions and is published widely in print and website collections. Johnmichael is chief editor of Cyclamens and Swords publishing and webmaster of *Voices: Israel group of poets in English* http://www.freewebs.com/voicesisrael/.

John Oliver Simon was awarded a National Endowment for the Arts Literary Fellowship in Translation in 2001 for his work with the great Chilean poet Gonzalo Rojas. One of Simon's poems is set in bronze in the sidewalk in the Addison Street Poetry Walk in his home town of Berkeley, California. His two-year-old granddaughter and muse, Tesla Rose Simon Moyer, is also the granddaughter of fellow contributor Linda Moyer.

Elaine Starkman writes both poetry and prose, often about family. Her earliest work was <u>Learning to Sit in the Silence: A Journal of Caretaking</u>, a memoir-diary of her mother-in-law coming to live with them. She also co-edited: <u>Here I Am: Contemporary Jewish Stories from Around the World</u>. Currently, she is co-editor of <u>My Dreaming Waking Life: Six Poets, Sixty-Six Poems</u>, a limited collection of six East Bay poets. Starkman has won prizes from the Benicia Love Poem Contest and the Ashville Writers Workshop in prose.

Parker Towle's full length book of poems, <u>This Weather Is No Womb</u> was published by Antrim House Books in 2007. He teaches at Dartmouth.

Karen Waggoner is the author of <u>On My Honor, A Navy Wife's Vietnam War</u>, selected as the first place winner in the Ozark Creative Writers book competition in 2005. In addition, several of her essays and short stories have been published in anthologies and periodicals, both by Ozark Writers' League and by independent publishers. She has been a fellow of the National Writing Project since 1985.

Donna Wahlert has published her poetry in anthologies such as *Mothers and Daughters: A Poetry Celebration, Heal Your Soul, Heal the World, Proposing on the Brooklyn Bridge, Animal Blessings, Wedding Blessings, Bless the Beasts Children's Book, Sunlight on the Moon, Hidden Roots, The Magnetic Poetry Book of Poetry, Still Waters, Lyrical Iowa, Christmas Blessings, On Retirement: 75 Poems, Miracles of Motherhood, To Have and to Hold.* She has appeared in journals such as *Kalliope, Calyx, Thema, Slant, Sistersong: Women Across Cultures, Mediphors, Earth's Daughters, Lifeboat, Verve, Palo Alto Review, 100 Words, Poets On: Complaints, Poets on: Twentieth Anniversary Reprise, Tucson Poet, Julien's Journal.* She has also published a collection of her poetry, <u>The First Pressing: Poetry of the Everyday</u>. She was a nominee for a 1995 Pushcart Prize Award, a winner of the Mary Blake Finan Literary Award in Poetry from Clarke College and was awarded first place in poetry by the Gulf Coast Chapter of the American's Writers' Association.

Child of my Child

Made in the USA
Lexington, KY
08 December 2010